A CRY

from the

FAR
MIDDLE

ALSO BY P. J. O'ROURKE

Modern Manners
An Etiquette Book for Rude People

The Bachelor Home Companion
A Practical Guide to Keeping House Like a Pig

Republican Party Reptile
Confessions, Adventures, Essays, and (Other) Outrages

Holidays in Hell
*In Which Our Intrepid Reporter Travels to the World's Worst Places
and Asks, "What's Funny About This?"*

Parliament of Whores
A Lone Humorist Attempts to Explain the Entire U.S. Government

Give War a Chance
*Eyewitness Accounts of Mankind's Struggle Against Tyranny, Injustice,
and Alcohol-Free Beer*

All the Trouble in the World
*The Lighter Side of Overpopulation, Famine, Ecological Disaster,
Ethnic Hatred, Plague, and Poverty*

Age and Guile Beat Youth, Innocence, and a Bad Haircut
"I Was Tragically Hip and I Recovered! You Can Too!"

Eat the Rich
A Treatise on Economics

The CEO of the Sofa
*One Year in the Life of a Man Who Said, "Mind If I Put My Feet Up?
I Think I Will Take This Lying Down."*

Peace Kills
America's Fun New Imperialism

On the Wealth of Nations
A Minor Mister Opines upon a Master's Magnum Opus

Driving Like Crazy
*Thirty Years of Vehicular Hell-Bending Celebrating America the Way It's Supposed
to Be—With an Oil Well in Every Backyard, a Cadillac Escalade in Every Carport,
and the Chairman of the Federal Reserve Mowing Our Lawn*

Don't Vote—It Just Encourages the Bastards
A Treatise on Politics

Holidays in Heck
A Former War Correspondent Experiences Frightening Vacation Fun

The Baby Boom
*How It Got That Way . . . And It Wasn't
My Fault . . . And I'll Never Do It Again*

Thrown Under the Omnibus
A Reader

How the Hell Did This Happen?
The Election of 2016

None of My Business
*P.J. Explains Money, Banking, Debt, Equity, Assets, Liabilities,
and Why He's Not Rich and Neither Are You*

A CRY

from the

FAR
MIDDLE

DISPATCHES
from a
DIVIDED
LAND

P. J.
O'ROURKE

Grove Press
New York

Earlier versions of a number of chapters in this book originally
appeared in the online magazine *American Consequences*

Published simultaneously in Canada
Printed in the United States of America

This book was set in 12.5-pt. ITC Berkely Oldstyle
by Alpha Design & Composition of Pittsfield, NH.

First Grove Atlantic hardcover edition: September 2020
First Grove Atlantic paperback edition: September 2021

Library of Congress Cataloging-in-Publication data available for this title.

ISBN 978-0-8021-5774-4
eISBN 978-0-8021-5775-1

Grove Press
an imprint of Grove Atlantic
154 West 14th Street
New York, NY 10011

Distributed by Publishers Group West

groveatlantic.com

21 22 23 24   10 9 8 7 6 5 4 3 2 1

To Andrew Ferguson

*Great writer, great friend, great guide in
the political wilderness with whom I have explored
the savage land of the Yahoos and with whom I still hope
to discover the lost country of the Houyhnhnms*

"Clowns to the left of me, jokers to the right,
Here I am, stuck in the middle with you."

—Stealers Wheel

CONTENTS

Pre-Preface:
As We Go to Press . . .

While this book was being written in 2019, America was deep in an era of idiot populism and hooligan partisanship.

Our country was engaged in a sort of socio-political Peloponnesian War. That is, we were in the midst of a long, confusing, tedious, useless, foolish conflict that threatened to destroy democracy and left ordinary commonsensical people feeling "It's all Greek to me."

Then, when this book was being edited and typeset, somebody ate an undercooked bat in a Wuhan wet market.

Panic and pandemic ensued. The nation was brought to a stay-at-home standstill—whether reasonably or not no one is quite certain and by whose authority no one is quite sure. "It's like being sixteen again," a friend of mine said. "Gas is cheap and I'm grounded."

Then, with everyone cooped up, going crazy and going broke, some fussbudget with a loose mutt in Central Park calls 911—"There's an African American man threatening my life"—after being admonished by a Harvard-educated bird-watcher (who, if video is anything to go by, is the very picture of a Harvard-educated bird-watcher).

On the same day as that Central Park display of American inclusiveness and mutual respect, members of the Minneapolis police force decide to take a knee—on the neck of George Floyd. After nearly nine minutes of suffocation, Floyd died. He was accused of spending twenty dollars in the form of a banknote that had no actual value. The U.S. Senate and House of Representatives are currently spending billions of dollars in the form of banknotes that have no actual value. Would the police employ the same bigotry and violence on them?

No. All across the country the police would employ bigotry and violence on people protesting the bigotry and violence of the police.

Chaos cried out its appeal. The thievish and the vandalistic are friends of chaos, and when their friend calls they come.

The president of the United States called for peace, understanding, and unity. In a pig's ass he did. The president waddled down to his bunker hidey-hole under the White House and urged the U.S. military to invade the country they live in. Then he talked trash and went to church (he could use it) attacking thousands of non-violent demonstrators to get there (not a very Christian way of going to church).

That's where things stood as this book made its—socially distancing and peacefully protesting—way to the printer.

All this is to say that my book looks back on an era of troubles that, in retrospect, seem to have been the good old days.

And now I—who have covered politics and all its works and all its empty promises for half a century and who had so very many things to say about them—am left mute.

There are people possessed of the expertise necessary to explain, analyze, and make judicious commentary upon the present and future effects of the novel coronavirus. And there are, I suppose, people endowed with the foresight to determine the outcome of the social upheavals accompanying the pandemic. I'm not one of either of them.

And the last thing the world needs at the moment is more pundits who don't know what they're talking about.

Journalists are supposed to provide answers. But all I've got is questions.

Starting with, isn't somebody supposed to be in charge?

Too many of America's elected leaders have been acting as if the pandemic is a children's party game where they're all blindfolded and swinging sticks—except they're clobbering each other instead of the virus piñata.

Under microscopic view coronavirus *does* look like it would make a swell papier-mâché target full of . . . lethal pathogens. Let's leave the politicians to amuse themselves while we skip this fiesta.

Which raises another question—about this book itself. Is it now completely beside the point?

Will American politics be fundamentally changed by the pandemic? Will Americans emerge from their grievous health crisis, lock-down isolation, economic collapse, and material depravation with a newly calm, pragmatic, and reasonable attitude toward our political system? Will our reawakened awareness of systemic prejudice cause us to critically analyze and democratically restrain our civil institutions? Will we abandon the factional hysterias and histrionics of the early twenty-first century in favor of a polity based upon competence, civil discourse, and good will?

Or will we revert to our petty arguments and stupid animadversions? Having had time alone to dwell on our grievances and affronts, will we maybe even return to our spiteful quarreling with renewed vigor? This is often how human nature works.

I'm betting that human nature will triumph over adversity and challenge. And I don't mean that in a good way.

—P. J. O'R.
June 8, 2020

Preface:
Manifesto For
Extreme Moderation

A Voice of the Political Far-Middle

What this country needs is fewer people who know what this country needs. We'd be better off, in my opinion, without so many opinions. Especially without so many political opinions. Including my own.

Our nation faces a multitude of difficult, puzzling, complex, and abstruse problems. Most Americans aren't sure what to do about them. But we lack politicians with the courage to say, "I'm not sure what to do about them either." We even lack politicians with the courage to say, "I'm not sure what 'abstruse' means."

Our economy has been upended by technological changes that make the industrial revolution look like James Watt putting a bigger teakettle on a hotter stove.

Our second Gilded Age, with its golden pathways across the ether, is a goldbrick when it comes to crumbling roads, decaying bridges, rackety public transit, corroding water pipes, and collapsing sewers.

A soaring economy has left absurd deprivation in the midst of ridiculous luxury. A click on a website can now deliver everything to everybody—except a living wage.

Meanwhile we're undergoing social changes so swift and profound that they send even the best cultural anthropologist fleeing. A latter-day Margaret Mead would be hiding out in Samoa, hoping like heck to study something as relatively uncomplicated as teenagers.

The tic-tac-toe of Cold War diplomacy has given way to the foreign policy conundrums of tri-dimensional chess, like Captain Kirk and Mr. Spock played on the starship *Enterprise*, except the pawns have nukes.

Transformations in health care have turned the historically cheapest part of being alive—dying—into something so expensive that many people can't afford to do it.

And surviving Americans are left trying to weigh the delicate balance between having a life worth living and having a planet that can support life.

Yet our political leaders all think they know the answer to "What Is to Be Done?," to quote Vladimir Lenin, a political leader who—among his other faults—flunked his own quiz.

The problem with opinions is that they're not synonymous with accomplishing anything. I have three school-age children with strong opinions about climate change but who can't remember to close the front door in midwinter. The traditional dad line, "We're not heating the outdoors," hasn't worked, so I appeal to their wokeness: "That would cause global warming!"

Then I drag the snow blower in from the garage to clear the front hall.

We need a political system that isn't so darn sure of itself. It's time for the rise of the extreme moderate. Power to the far-middle! Let's bring the Wishy and the Washy back together, along with the Namby and the Pamby, and the Milque and the Toast.

The extreme moderates' non-negotiable demand? Negotiation. We won't compromise until we see some compromising. We want political action . . . or inaction . . . it depends.

And wouldn't it be great if we had an opinion-free news media source? I have the perfect name for it, "Happy Medium."

We may be on different sides of the fence, but let's make that fence-top wider and better padded and go sit on it. Then, no matter if I'm of conservative ilk and you're of liberal stripe, we can have a neighborly chat.

Should the government be Laissez? Should the government be Faire?

We're all in favor of peace, but when the wolf dwells with the lamb and the leopard lies down with the kid, how often do we have to replace those sheep and goats?

Does Medicare for All mean young people have to wear trifocals and Depends and trade their bicycles for walkers?

If taxpayer money is used to pay for political campaigns, do taxpayers have ninety days to return politicians for a full refund?

Animal rights are important, but what about animal responsibilities?

Does "Pursuit of Happiness" mean I can drink before noon?

These are all important questions. Let's discuss them while making social justice more sociable. Here, have a nip from my hip flask. We might be able to come to some accommodation with each other's views.

If today's political leaders would rather burn the milquetoast and ignore the wishes of the wishy-washy, extreme moderates should hang them out with the wash and they'll be toast. Mixed-metaphorically speaking, of course, because harsh words and rash actions are not our style.

Indeed, how to go about being an extreme moderate presents some problems. The kind of things that other extremists do seem so . . . extreme. But I do have one idea. Free speech should not only be protected, it should be compulsory.

Everyone with a strong political opinion should be required to wear a sign proclaiming it.

Hang an "Immigration Is Ruining America" placard around your neck and see how you get treated by restaurant staff, Uber drivers, the people who change your hotel linen, and your immigrant grandparents.

Go see your personal physician with "I Want the Government to Run Your Doctor's Office" lettered in Magic Marker across your abdomen. "Sorry, Senator Warren, but it looks like we're going to have to remove your *other* appendix."

Introduction:
O Beautiful for . . . Pilgrim Feet?

America is in need of some explaining, especially at the moment.

That the country is a mess is the one thing the country agrees on. And even about this we differ. Half the nation seems to be saying, "We don't know what's wrong with America, but we can fix it," while the other half says, "There's nothing wrong with America, and we can fix *that*."

Polar icecaps may be melting (or not!) but America's polarization is frozen solid. And if the climate itself is a contentious issue then we cannot so much as agree on what the weather's like outside.

Everything is much more wrong than it ever was, and we are much more right about it. We're all mad at each other and incensed that others are furious with us. It's a sort of permanent anti-Christmas, an obligatory holiday exchange where we're bound to receive umbrage and compelled to give offense.

Everybody's got a beef. Except the vegans, they've got a Beyond Meat. To tally our national complaints would be to empty a bathtub with a spoon. And after this long and sodden labor we'd find some new tangle of combover hairs in the political drain or ring of scum on the social porcelain that we hadn't thought to complain about before. It is confusion.

And, lest this most general of statements escape bitter contention, the previous sentence was—trigger warning (or is "trigger warning" an implicit denial of Second Amendment rights?)—a quotation from the Bible, Leviticus 18:23, forbidding sex with animals.

Further topics for Twitter storms: Is Leviticus 18:23 blatant anthropocentrism or a swipe left on Tinder? Does Leviticus also forbid sex with plant protein based–beef substitutes even when they are free from GMOs, soy, and gluten? Is posting the gluten content in communion wafers a threat to religious freedoms?

We have worked ourselves into a state of angry perplexity.

Not that this is anything new. America was discovered with angry perplexity. In 1524 a perplexed Giovanni da Verrazzano—an Italian explorer serving the king of France by mapping what would become British colonies —mistook the shallow waters west of North Carolina's Outer Banks for the Pacific Ocean. Subsequent navigators, finding the dunes of Cape Hatteras rather than the riches of the Orient, were angry.

And America was founded in angry perplexity, starting with the first attempt to colonize the nation, on those Outer Banks, at the "lost colony" of Roanoke.

The people who already lived on Roanoke Island, the Croatoan and the Dasamongueponke, were perplexed when 115 English arrived uninvited in 1587. Angry, too. Within a few days the Dasamongueponke had killed one of the English, George Howe. Within a few more days the English had killed several of the Croatoan who'd had nothing to do with Howe's death.

Thus a precedent was set for the way different kinds of Americans would treat each other for the next four hundred–some years and what would happen to innocent bystanders when the treatment was being handed out. (Advice to American bystanders: don't stand *by*, stand *back*.)

Any number of horrifying examples can be cited, from the first colonial legislation legally recognizing slavery in 1641 (in enlightened, nominally pro-emancipation Massachusetts) to the "battle" of Wounded Knee in 1890 (several hundred Lakota casualties, mostly women, children, and old men) to the choke-hold killing of Eric Garner in Staten Island in 2014. (He died after being apprehended by police for selling loose cigarettes in violation of New York's strict legislation to limit the harmful effects of tobacco.)

I quote the late Christopher Hitchens, "History is a tragedy and not a morality tale."

But the precedent the Roanoke colonists *thought* they were setting was more like the gentrification of Brooklyn. Not that innocent bystanders haven't been harmed in Bushwick—priced out of their humble abodes so that craft kombucha brewers, aspiring mobile app developers, Anusara yoga practitioners, and indie musicians who drive part-time for Uber could move in.

Traveling to Roanoke in 1587 were eighty-nine men, seventeen women, and nine children (including, we must assume, at least a couple of adolescents muttering, "*This sucks*"). They were Londoners—tradesmen, artisans, and their families. The venture was a sixteenth-century version of a real estate investment trust. The REIT had a charter from Queen Elizabeth that formed a corporation headed by Sir Walter Raleigh (comfortably back in England).

The colonists hoped to become genteel, to attain the status of landed gentry. Although the gentleman managing the scheme, the governor of the Roanoke Colony, John White, was a member of the gentry by virtue of being a celebrated watercolor artist.

As far as scholars can tell, the colonists had estate management skills and agricultural expertise about equal to indie musicians in Brooklyn. Or not even, given the musicians' cannabis grow rooms. And while Roanoke Colony did become a "gated community" after George Howe was killed, there were no provisions for organized security or defense.

Besides not getting along with their new neighbors, in whose backyards they were camping, the colonists had angry perplexities of their own. The expedition was so poorly provisioned that within a month of their arrival the colonists petitioned Governor White to return to England for more supplies.

He didn't get back until three years later. Some things came up. A 1588 relief mission was distracted by a side hustle in privateering and a fight with French pirates near Morocco, which to a modern sailor with GPS would be very much in the wrong direction from North Carolina. Then there was the Spanish Armada. Seafaring watercolor artists were needed on the home front.

When the governor of the Roanoke Colony finally landed back on Roanoke Island his colony was gone. All that was left was an abandoned palisade with the word "Croatoan" carved on a post.

White took this to mean that the colonists had moved to the nearby island called Croatoan or, perhaps, had made some Airbnb arrangements with the Croatoans, who were friendly to the English. Or they had been friendly until they were mistaken for Dasamongueponkes and killed. Maybe Croatoans were friendly again.

White meant to go find out. But some other things came up. One of his ships wanted to go home. The other broke an anchor cable and was blown so far off course, with White aboard, that it came ashore in the Azores.

As long as his Roanoke colonists were not proven to be dead, Sir Walter Raleigh could maintain his corporate claim on what was loosely called "Virginia" (everything on the continent north of Spanish Florida). This may cast doubt on the complete sincerity of Raleigh's claim to have been trying to find them on his 1595 voyage to the New World while he was also searching for El Dorado.

No other major effort to locate the Roanoke colonists was made until after the Jamestown Colony was established in 1607, and by then there was no trace.

No one knows what happened to the residents of the Lost Colony. I think that, full of angry perplexity, they stomped off in a huff.

Which set another precedent for America. People do not emigrate because things are going well at home.

This was true for ancient migrants from Asia 20,000 years ago. Or 30,000 years ago or 40,000 years ago—there is fractious conflict about that too. Geologists, paleontologists, archaeologists, and anthropologists turn out to be as polarized as the rest of us. (Fortunately their lengthy scientific terms pretty much keep their angry perplexities from being aired on Twitter.)

Nonetheless, there was some time when some people headed over the Bering Strait land bridge waving farewell. "See you later, you frozen Siberians with your itchy woolly mammoth long underwear and mastodon meat on your breath. We're off to the beautiful Pacific Northwest—waterfront property, split-level longhouses, decorative totem pole lawn ornaments, and salmon frying on the barbecue grill!"

Then—midst weekend sightseeing jaunts to watch the glaciers retreat and hunting trips to bag soon-to-be-extinct trophy megafauna—they proceeded to have their own Roanoke Colony moments. Never mind that there wasn't anybody else already living in the New World to quarrel with.

In November 2015 *National Geographic* published an article by Glenn Hodges, "First Americans," detailing "new finds, theories, and genetic discoveries" about the populating of the Western Hemisphere. (Given the current animosity surplus, I'm sure somebody's mad at *National Geographic* too, because of cultural appropriation, or because you have to be a member of the National Geographic Society to get the magazine so this is probably a secret society maybe funded by George Soros, or because an old, dead, white male had accumulated thirty years of back issues in the attic and these fell through the kitchen ceiling on the heads of the "Flip or Flop" TV crew, or *something*.)

Anyway, the article said:

> If you look at the skeletal remains of Paleo-Americans, more than half of the men have injuries caused by violence, and four out of ten have skull fractures. The wounds don't appear to have been the result of hunting mishaps, and they don't bear telltale signs of warfare, like blows suffered fleeing an attacker. Instead it appears that these men fought among themselves—often and violently. The women don't have these kinds of injuries, but they're much smaller than the men, with signs of malnourishment and domestic abuse.

Nor did the post-Roanoke Europeans find America to be a day at the beach. (Although George Howe was in fact having a day at the beach, gathering crabs, when the Dasamongueponke shot him full of arrows.)

Unlike the 1587 Lost Colony's ex-residents, the 1607 Jamestown colonists weren't seeking status, just money.

Their flight from impoverishment in England amounted to a lethal version of a 1930s Warner Brothers animated cartoon gag. Depravation chased the colonists around the barn of poverty and they ran so hard and heedlessly that they collided with depravation's backside. Of the five hundred some colonists who arrived in Jamestown between 1607 and 1610, 440 of them died, mostly from starvation.

The initial settlers landed too late in the year to plant crops and didn't know much about planting anyway. Their only piece of good fortune was not being immediately evicted by the local landlords, the Powhatan Confederacy.

This was an organization of about thirty Algonquian-speaking tribes that had formed a military alliance against Siouan-speaking tribes to their north and west under the leadership of Wahunsenacawh, father of Pocahontas.

The Powhatan were well aware of the three rules of real estate. None of them lived on the location, location, location of Jamestown. The peninsula on the James River at the mouth of Chesapeake Bay was mosquito infested, too swampy for farming or hunting, and, wetland though it may have been, suffering a drought that left the colonists nothing to drink but brackish river water.

Having mentioned Pocahontas, we might pause to consider what we can learn about the founding of America from one of the few prefoundational Americans that we know something about.

Except we don't know anything about her, starting with her real name, which was Matoaka unless it was Amonute. She either saved the life of John Smith, one of the Jamestown expedition's original leaders, or she didn't. She may have been participating in an adoption ritual where her father pretended to club Smith on the head. She may not have been there at all. Smith didn't mention her in his first account of being captured by Wahunsena-cawh. Smith's stories about Pocahontas are inconsistent. He seems to be making them up as he goes along.

We're told in early histories of Jamestown that as a child Pocahontas sometimes visited the colony and was acquainted with John Smith. (John Smith? John White? The early history of America reads like the guest register at a shady motel.)

In 1613, after the English and the Powhatan had had a falling-out, Pocahontas was, in turn, captured (more like kidnapped) by the colonists. Perhaps she had Stockholm syndrome. Or a sadder story. She converted to Christianity, took yet another name, "Rebecca," married colonist John Rolfe, and had a son, Thomas.

Rolfe took her and Thomas to England where she was a minor celebrity, something short of a Wallis Simpson but considered more presentable to a king. And she was presented to King James. She lived near London for most of a year. In the one portrait of her rendered from life she looks a bit dour. (Probably the weather.) Then, after getting onboard a ship back to Virginia with her husband and son, she became ill and died at Gravesend, aged twenty or twenty-one.

Thomas survived, wed the daughter of a wealthy Virginia landowner, and had a daughter who married a Colonel Robert Bolling. A number of prominent Virginia families—including that of Woodrow Wilson's wife Edith (nee Bolling)—claim descent from Pocahontas. So we learn that American racism is, at least, topped by descended-from-a-princess snobbery. Pocahontas was the Meghan Markle of her day. Other than that we learn nothing. We might as well have watched the very stupid 1995 Disney movie.

The Jamestown colonists did not arrive with the equipment, supplies, or inclination to found a self-sustaining colony. The Jamestown business model was to export valuable commodities. But they couldn't find any. They shipped a load of clapboard to England.

The London investors who had funded Jamestown were not best pleased. They sent a stiff note along with their 1608 (inadequate) resupply of the colony. According to the historian James Horn, preeminent expert on Jamestown, the investors insisted that the colonists send them enough goods to pay for the cost of the resupply voyage plus a lump of gold, proof that the South Sea had been discovered, and somebody from the Lost Colony of Roanoke.

And a partridge in a pear tree.

Jamestown would go down in history—and down was the direction it was headed—for many American firsts. The kind of firsts you wish America hadn't had.

The poorest among the Jamestown colonists were the first to condemn themselves to indentured servitude to pay for their trip to America. Their terms of bondage ranged from three to seven years, but it was mostly death rather than time served that released them from their debt.

To add evil to iniquity, the first abducted Africans known to have been transported to British America were sold as slaves in Jamestown in 1619.

The same year brought America's first politicking and America's first elected assembly, Jamestown's Virginia House of Burgesses. The legislative body was founded "to establish one equal and uniform government over all Virginia" with "just laws for the happy guiding and governing of the people there inhabiting." Although to hell with the happy guiding of the Powhatan and every other un-English-born, un-male, un-free, un-Jamestown colony resident on the continent north of Spanish Florida. They weren't part of the electorate.

Also that same year Jamestown experienced America's first strike. The colony included a number of artisans who hadn't been born in England. They seem to have been the only artisans the colony possessed. They included a soap maker, a timber crafter, and a glass blower. They went on strike for the right to vote. And it may have been America's first (and last?) quick and amiable settlement between organized labor and management. Dirty Englishmen sitting under sagging roof beams drinking out of cupped hands immediately granted artisans the franchise.

The House of Burgesses legislated as wisely as American legislatures continue to do, that is, making laws that invited—nay, demanded—evasion. The first item passed by the House of Burgesses was an imposition of price controls on export produce.

The only produce being exported was tobacco, and the colonists were barely able to grow any of that. I'm sure they embraced the 1619 price controls with the same enthusiasm that, during the Gerald Ford administration, we all wore WIN buttons and fervently obeyed the injunctions of the "Whip Inflation Now" campaign.

The Jamestown colonists were the first Europeans to invade the inland of our nation, sending raiding parties up the James River to steal Powhatan crops and occupy Powhatan land. In 1622 the Powhatan Confederacy made the first successful large-scale, tactically coordinated attack on Europeans, killing 347 of them.

The colonists were pushed back into the original Jamestown fortifications. The Powhatan hoped the colony, if it remained at all, would be reduced to a small trading post. The Powhatan thought the colonists had been taught a lesson. The colonists—*not* a first—hadn't.

Warfare, sometimes acute, sometimes chronic, continued against ever more numerous and better-armed Jamestown forces. Meanwhile the colonists were deploying our country's first weapons of mass destruction. Although, to be fair, they didn't know that their germs and viruses even existed.

*   *   *

All the tales of American Indian fighter heroics (whether your hero is Crazy Horse or Davy Crockett) turn to ashes in the mouths of the tellers when facts are considered. The New World was conquered by coughs, sneezes, and craps in the woods.

The historian David Stannard, in his thoroughly disheartening book about the death and destruction of the Western Hemisphere's aboriginal inhabitants, *American Holocaust*, estimates that the Powhatan Confederacy numbered about 14,000 people when Jamestown was founded. But the germs had arrived before the germy. The region's population had already been reduced by diseases spreading from the first European contacts in the late fourteenth century, perhaps drastically reduced. By the end of the seventeenth century only about six hundred Powhatan were left, a mortality rate of more than 95 percent.

Germs were the A-bomb. The Indians were militarily skilled and fighting on their own turf. Without germs the British colonists would have met the same fate that the American colonists dealt the British a hundred years later.

And the U.S.A. would be a different country. (Although, given the demographic pressures in Europe, still plagued by illegal immigrants. But they'd be you and me.)

In 1677 a treaty established what amounted to America's first Indian reservation. This was land "reserved" for surviving members of the Powhatan Confederacy.

The Treaty of 1677 was honored the way treaty rights on Indian reservations continue to be—making fraud instead of fighting the way to get Powhatan land.

Jamestown also had America's first armed colonial uprising, Bacon's Rebellion, in 1676. Nathaniel Bacon was a rich spoiled young scoundrel from England whose father had kicked him out of the house and sent him packing to America (albeit with £1800 in walking around money). Nathaniel bought two plantations on the James River and got his rebellion named for himself by being elected leader after giving the other rebels a lot of brandy.

What they were rebelling against was the Jamestown colony governor William Berkeley who was either too friendly with (dangerous!) Native Americans or not friendly enough with them to get other Jamestown colonists in on the fur trade (lucrative!) with Native Americans. The issue is—as issues could get to be even before the Internet—confused.

One thing can be said in favor of the rebellion: it was inclusive. Indentured servants and slaves joined with plantation owners in rebelling. It's heartening to see Americans working together toward a common goal. Although that can also be said of the 1622 Powhatan attack.

Bacon had his rebels point their muskets at Governor Berkeley who (he may have been drinking brandy himself) bared his chest and told them to go ahead and shoot. So Bacon had his rebels point their muskets at the elected Burgesses who—every bit as courageous as today's House and Senate members—promptly gave in.

Although what they gave in *to* is not exactly clear. Anyway it wasn't enough because Bacon's rebels set fire to the House of Burgesses and the entire settlement burned.

Nathaniel Bacon died of diarrhea. Governor Berkeley returned to power in 1677. In yet another first, predating the Salem witch trial mass executions by fifteen years, he hanged twenty-three of the men who had rebelled against . . . the deep state, or whatever.

The Jamestown House of Burgesses was rebuilt but burned again, accidently. By 1699 Virginians had had enough of mosquito-infested, swampy, fractious, flammable Jamestown and moved their capital to Williamsburg. Or, as it is now known, "Colonial" Williamsburg.

Jamestown's last first would be to usher in the "living history" tourist trap at Williamsburg. This was America's initial foray into making its history cute—Disneyfication while Walt was still doodling mice.

Colonial Williamsburg was created in the 1920s by the kind of cross section of America that makes the rest of us Americans rather cross. Founders included the local Episcopal minister, the Daughters of the Confederacy, the Chamber of Commerce, and a group that went by (and still does) the marvelous name Colonial Dames. And the enterprise was paid for by John D. Rockefeller (whose own history of financial dealing was less than adorable).

A visit to Colonial Williamsburg is at least as informative as a meet and greet with Pocahontas at Disney

World. "Pocahontas will pose for photos with you and you can get her autograph. She appears daily at various times. Get the Animal Kingdom guide for exact times during your visit."

If John D. had read more American history (his higher education was a ten-week business course at Folsom's Commercial College in Cleveland), he wouldn't have picked this part of it for "living."

Or maybe—he was a man of foresight—he would have. Right now America seems determined to relive its early history in every detail of angry perplexity—from Verrazzano-like trade war confusion about the riches of the Orient, to calling Elizabeth Warren Pocahontas, to an endlessly woke Bacon-type rebellion against everything and nothing, to blog threats to hang antifas from alt-right wannabe Governor Berkeleys on 4chan.

Thus, in explaining America, the "Ain't it awful" explanation is always available, if we want it.

Ravaged by climate change. Torn by internecine strife. Gross inequality in the distribution of wealth. Widespread poverty. Drug use. Oppression of women and minorities.

And that was in 1491. Next year things got much worse.

Can't we choose some other moment in the American chronology to live our living history life in? Surely there was a time when America was in flower, at peace with itself and the world, growing in prosperity and hope, with shared values, respected institutions, and confident love of country. You know, the "Great" that's the "Again" in the "Make America . . ." thing.

Maybe that moment would be about 1910 when "America the Beautiful" became a popular patriotic song. It's a stirring tune. Many are of the opinion that it should be our national anthem. It's much easier to sing than "The Star-Spangled Banner." Even Roseanne Barr couldn't butcher it in front of 50,000 irked baseball fans in San Diego at the 1990 Padres–Cincinnati Reds game. (Padres owner Tom Werner was the producer of the *Roseanne* sitcom—in case you've been wondering WTF? for thirty years.) Some find "The Star-Spangled Banner" too bellicose. Others think it contains a coded message advocating open borders ("Jose can you see . . .") Anyway, nobody ever takes a knee on "*And crown thy good with brotherhood.*"

But "America the Beautiful" is not so anodyne or naïf as it seems. Its lyricist certainly wasn't. Katharine Lee Bates (1859–1929) studied at Wellesley College and Oxford. She was the head of the English Department at Wellesley, neither then nor now a nest of conservative complacency. She was a formidable social activist supporting women's suffrage, world peace, unionized labor, slum clearance, poor relief, and immigrant rights. She traveled the world and was a war correspondent for the *New York Times* during the Spanish-American War, which, as all politically correct people did at the time, she deplored. She was a friend of Carl Sandburg, Robert Frost, and William Butler Yeats, as well as a widely published

poet herself. Though not, truth to tell, a very good one.
Sample this verse from her "In a Northern Wood":

> FRAGRANT *are the cedar-boughs stretching green and level,*
> *Feasting-halls where waxwings flit at their spicy revel,*
> *But O the pine, the questing pine, that flings its arms on high*
> *To search the secret of the sun and escalade the sky!*

Bates, however, was also a lifelong Republican and
quit the GOP in 1924 only because of the party's refusal
to support the League of Nations. Furthermore she may
have been gay, sharing a home for twenty-five years with
fellow Wellesley professor Katharine Coman. If we are
looking for a representative of a simpler time and place,
Katharine Lee Bates is the wrong example.

She wrote the words to "America the Beautiful" first
as a poem in 1893. (The music it would be set to in 1910
was from an 1882 hymn by the organist and composer
Samuel Ward.) Bate's poem was inspired by a transcon-
tinental train journey from Boston by way of Chicago
and Denver to Pikes Peak. To begin with let us recall that
trains, before they arrive at purple mountain majesties,
don't pass through the best parts of town.

Now sing along with me. And let's pay close attention to what Bates is saying.

> *O beautiful for spacious skies,*
> *For amber waves of grain,*
> *For purple mountain majesties*

Only one out of three of which Americans can take any credit for.

> *Above the fruited plain!*

KLB was perfectly aware of the deplorable working conditions of fruit pickers.

> *America! America!*
> *God shed* [Odd word choice. Like a dog sheds? America could use more God on its furniture?] *His grace on thee*
> *And crown* [sixth definition, Webster's, "to hit on the head"] *thy good with brotherhood*
> *From sea to shining sea!*
>
> *O beautiful for pilgrim* [whose arrival on the *Mayflower* would nowadays be called Christian Right activism] *feet,*
> *Whose stern impassioned stress*

Like other Puritan groups, the pilgrims would be the source of considerable stress in America.

> *A thoroughfare for freedom beat*
> *Across the wilderness.*

KLB is putting things tactfully here. It was the germs from the pilgrim's *dirty* feet that beat the thoroughfare.

America! America!
God mend thine every flaw,

Implying a tailoring job for the ages.

Confirm thy soul in self-control,

KLB was a Congregationalist, and the Congregational Church was an important force in the temperance movement.

Thy liberty in law.

Which law KLB wanted to change in a variety of ways.

O beautiful for heroes proved
In liberating strife,

When explaining America, "liberating strife" is one way to put it.

Who more than self their country loved

KLB flatters us.

And mercy more than life!

But here she goes too far.

America! America!
May God thy gold refine,

Advocacy for "hard money" gold standard? KLB *was* a Republican.

Till all success be nobleness,

But she was also offended by the excesses of the Gilded Age.

And every gain divine!

Still, as mentioned, she was a Republican.

O beautiful for patriot dream
That sees beyond the years

The poem was written during the Panic of 1893, a severe economic depression that lasted until 1897.

Thine alabaster cities gleam
Undimmed by human tears!

KLB knew full well what dimmed the cities of America. Her reference here is to Chicago's World's Columbian Exposition of 1893, which she presumably saw on her trip west. Temporary buildings representing an optimistic future were sheathed in fine-grained gypsum.

America! America!
God shed [There He goes again. This time a snakeskin
     comes to mind.] *His grace on thee*

And crown [not to say clobber] *thy good with brotherhood*
From sea to shining sea!

What is America? Do other nations need this much
explaining?

Ask, "What is England?" and you'll get an earful from
the Bard by way of *Richard II*:

This royal throne of kings, this sceptred isle,
This earth of majesty, this seat of Mars,
This other Eden, demi-paradise,

. . .

This happy breed of men, this little world,
This precious stone set in the silver sea . . .

Aw, shut your hole.

Ask, "What is China?" and invite a long, boring lecture from sinologists or, worse, from Xi Jinping.

"What is France?" Prepare yourself for a load of brie,
and in French at that.

"What is Russia?" Churchill said it's "a riddle, wrapped
in a mystery, inside an enigma" and I'd add locked in a
jail cell and dumped in a shithole.

And let's not ask "What is Germany?" for fear that
they'll show us again.

Other nations are based on battle, blood, ethnicity, culture, language, and (unlike Jamestown) terra firma. Not

America. We're strangers turned loose in an opportunity. An opportunity to treat other strangers like shit very much included.

Witness, in the Declaration of Independence, our unalienable right to Pursuit of Happiness. Whatever the hell happiness is supposed to mean. *Pace* Webster's, "dominantly agreeable emotion ranging in value from mere contentment to deep and intense joy in living," happiness has no definition. Whatever makes you happy. We are a pursuit without a purpose. Always on the go with no idea where.

America is not a place. It was the middle of no place when people first got here and somebody else's place we're taking ever since. America is not an ideal, or lightning would have struck us dead long ago. America is not an idea either. Or if it is an idea, it's a fuzzy one. And we've always been of two (or 327.2 million) minds about it.

A friend of mine recently told me that America's angry perplexity made him feel confused. (Admittedly he's a cisgender hetronormative middle-aged white male from the Midwest and can't be expected to truly have *feelings*.) "I don't get it," he said. "America emerged from the Cold War with a military that dominates the world and an economy that does the same and now business is booming. Why aren't we taking a victory lap? Why aren't we fat and happy?"

Well, we've got the fat part . . .

* * *

Maybe we should just stick with the "Ain't it awful" explanation of America. When things don't turn out exactly the way we want, it's sort of comforting to think that they never did. Or maybe we should go with the "foreigner" explanation of America—a capitalistic, imperialistic, hegemonistic, grossly materialistic place rife with social and economic injustice where they all want to live.

Both true enough. Yet there's an "exceptional" explanation of America that's just as true and much more puzzling. Our country was founded by the delusional and the crazy, populated by the desperate and the unwilling, motivated by most of the Seven Deadly Sins, and is somehow . . . the richest and most powerful nation on earth, ever.

Which leads us to the "drunk" explanation of America. We'll let some drunk shout it from the back of the bar.

"We had to fuck a lot of people to make this baby!"

One Nation—Divided As Hell

How divided is America? We're so divided we can't agree on *anything*. Political debate is dominated by Left-Wing Kooks, Right-Wing Nuts, and Random Flakes. Show them the words of wisdom from America's (founding fathers) in *the Declaration of Independence* and *the Preamble to the Constitution* and they'll start screaming at each other—and at us.

Sexist! Chauvinist! Patriarchal! Cisgender normative!

Below, Left-Wing Kook ravings are shown in *kooky* typeface, Right-Wing Nut rants in **nutso** typeface, and Random Flake blathers in a **blitherblather** font.

No fake news in 1776!

Are pigs! #MeToo

We hold these (truths) to be

To dead white males

(self-evident), that all (men) are

Creationism proved!

Slave-owning hypocrites wrote the Declaration! Reparations now!

(created) (equal), that they are

Flat tax!

Trigger warning! Religious Right!

endowed by their (Creator) with

Build the wall!

The Redcoats were invaders from Mars!

certain (unalienable) (Rights), that

Second Amendment rights!

Overturn *Roe v. Wade!*

White skin privilege!

among these are (Life), (Liberty),

Gun control now!

Free the Dreamers!

Get off my lawn!

and the pursuit of (Happiness).

Legalize cannabis!

Flying ponies, unicorns, and candy-flavored rainbows!

Hillary won the popular vote!

School strike for climate!

No justice, no peace!

Medicare for All!

Ban domestic violence!

Universal Basic Income!

Ban the bomb!

Welfare rights!

Rising sea levels kill children!

AmeriKKKa!

We the (People) of the United States, in (Order) to form a more perfect (Union), establish (Justice), (insure) (domestic) (Tranquility), (provide) for the common (defense), promote the general (Welfare), and secure the (Blessings) of Liberty to ourselves and our (Posterity), do ordain and establish this Constitution for the United States of (America).

And plants and animals

New World Order! Black helicopters! Illuminati!

Deep state!

Jail Pelosi! Stop the impeachment coup!

As in the Sea of Tranquility . . . The moon landing was a hoax!

Nuke the UN!

Visualize Whirled Peas!

Get a job!

God, Guts & Guns!

My cat was Shirley MacLaine in a previous lifetime!

Make it You-Know-What Again!

Coastals vs. Heartlanders

They know all about organic, sustainable, non-GMO, pesticide-free, fair-traded, locavore, artisanal, gluten-free, hypoallergenic, and vegan. But they don't know hay from straw.

They are the Coastals—the enlightened, the progressive, the sensitive, the inclusive, the hip, the aware, the woke. They inhabit the metropolises of the Left Coast and the Eastern Seaboard from the Chesapeake Bay to Bar Harbor and they dwell in the trending atolls in between. You find them in Ann Arbor, Michigan; Austin, Texas; Boulder, Colorado; Taos, New Mexico, and all the other places where the smell of pot and $5 cups of coffee is stronger than the smell of factory smoke, crop fertilizer, heavy equipment diesel fumes, or the sweat of physical labor.

The opposite of Coastal is Heartland. As far as the people of the Heartland are concerned, you can tell Coastals from Heartlanders the way you can tell

Theories from practices

Ideas from actions

Words from deeds

The Harvard football team from the Ohio State
Buckeyes

The defining feature of Coastals is that they *know* so
much more than Heartlanders do. (Ignoring, of course,
Coastals feeding straw to the horse and trying to sip a
Starbucks Cascara Cold Foam through a blade of hay.)

The Coastals know what's good for the Heartlanders
better than the Heartlanders do. They know what's good
for the whole world better than the whole world does.
And the Coastals can prove it. It's a bad old world. So
the world must not know what the Coastals know or
the world would be good. It's not. Case closed.

Another defining feature of Coastals is that they *care*
so much more than Heartlanders do. They say to Okla-
homans, "Oh, sure, you care about climate change. But
you care only because of lawn-watering restrictions. We
really care. We care so much we quit using the toilet. And
because we care so much more than you do we're better
people than you are. The world should be run by better
people. Therefore we'll run Oklahoma from Washington."

Besides knowing and caring, a third defining feature
of Coastals is that they are so much more *successful* than
Heartlanders are. Materially, of course, but successful in
their attainment of righteousness as well. Hearlanders
try to be righteous, and almost always fail at it (just
go to one of their cement-block churches and listen
to one of their fire-and-brimstone preachers tell them

so). Coastals try to be *self*-righteous and they succeed every time.

As noted, being a Coastal or a Heartlander isn't purely a matter of geography. Although it's interesting to consider why Coastals dominate the coasts. Or some of the coasts. Coastals are scarce on the Gulf Coast, uncommon on the shores of the Great Lakes, and dominate the Atlantic Coast only as far south as Washington's Virginia suburbs. Hawaii is both lower case c and capital C Coastal, while Alaska has lots of coast but is almost entirely Heartland.

The Pacific Coast can be explained by a Midwestern saying: "Every now and then the country gets tilted and everything that's loose rolls out to California." As for New Yorkers, Bostonians, and their ilk, maybe while the rest of the nation was engaged in Manifest Destiny and the Great Western Migration the Northeast simply missed the bus.

But there are lonely Heartlanders in Berkeley and isolated Coastals frantically seeking their "safe space" in Tulsa.

The Heartland/Costal divide does not fall along strict lines of political ideology either. Harry Truman was a Heartlander. Steve Bannon makes Heartlander tornado noises but is in fact a Coastal hurricane of know-it-all, cared-stiff self-regard. Donald Trump is a Coastal pretending to be a Heartlander, covering his oh-so-Coastal real estate scammer face with a mask of drunk-in-a-bowling-alley Heartlander bigotry. Elizabeth Warren is a Heartlander. You can tell by the middle-American banality of all her "to-do" lists. These may be posted with Noam Chomsky, Paul Krugman, John Kenneth Galbraith, and Emma Goldman refrigerator magnets. But you know that, inside the fridge, is Miracle Whip, Velveeta, Spam, yellow mustard, iceberg lettuce, Jello salad, tuna casserole, meat loaf surprise made with Hamburger Helper, and leftover SpaghettiOs. Meanwhile, Bernie Sanders, with an almost identical political platform, has spent fifty-two years in the Heartland of Vermont and you could still use his New York accent to grate cheddar.

Nor are ethnic, racial, gender, sexual orientation, or religious "identities" determinative. Justice Scalia—Heartland. Sacco and Vanzetti—Coastal. Likewise: Colin Powell/Ta-Nehisi Coates, Peter Thiel/Rosie O'Donnell, Milton Friedman/Chuck Schumer.

Caitlyn Jenner is a Heartland jock. Former *Transparent* star Jeffrey Tambor is a Coastal snowflake. And, speaking of sexual harassment, #MeToo also spans the Coastal-Heartland divide. Bill Clinton is a Heartlander *and* a Tit-and-Asslander. (While Hillary is a doughy Heartlander full of flakey Coastal pretensions.)

Coastals are not all flakes. Among them there is an upper crust—crumbs that stick together.

Some sit atop the pie of finance. Heartlanders may make money, but Coastals *create* money in their opaque central banks, their arcane derivative markets, and their mystifying high-tech IPO offerings.

Some crumbs coat the bread loaf of politics. The political Coastals are devoted to social justice—a large pile of benefits to be distributed to the Heartland many, just as soon as the Coastal few have grabbed and hoarded a large pile of their own.

The political Coastals are enamored of world peace, although it's Coastals who send the U.S. military on fool's errands to Iraq and Afghanistan. It's Heartlanders who join up.

The crux of the matter is not about Heartlanders being good and Coastals being evil. It's about their respective ability to tell the difference.

This is similar to their respective judgments about intoxication at an early age. Young Heartlanders get drunk and know they've become stupid. Young Coastals get stoned and think they've become brilliant. The same pattern will continue into adulthood. Mature Heartlanders watch the news about something like the 2020 presidential election and know they've become confused. Mature Coastals watch the same news about the same something and think they've become experts.

Heartlanders believe in applying common sense to the question of good and evil. Coastals believe in arguing the premises of the question.

To take a simple example of good, there's the Bill of Rights. A Heartlander looks at the Bill of Rights and thinks, "It's pretty good." A Coastal has an argument with every one of the first ten Amendments.

I. Free speech
What if it makes college students cry?

II. Right to bear arms
Unless the guns are scary-looking.

III. No soldiers to be quartered in houses in time of peace
Does Airbnb count? Because Airbnb is contributing to the shortage of affordable housing in rapidly gentrifying inner cities and while I don't advocate the quartering of soldiers per se, because that might be insensitive to antiwar home owners, there are the homeless to be considered and . . .

IV. Unlawful search and seizure
Although in many ways Wikileaks made important contributions to the goals of transparency in . . .

V. Protection against self-incrimination
Unless investigated by the House of Representatives Judiciary Committee.

VI. & VII. Right to jury trial
When not already found guilty in a New York Times *editorial.*

VIII. Prohibition of cruel and unusual punishment
Except reputational death by Twitter.

IX. Enumerated rights
Wait a minute! They left out the right to health care, the right to education, the right to a living wage, the right to . . .

X. **"The Powers not delegated to the United States by the Constitution, nor prohibited by it to the States, are reserved to the States respectively, or to the people."**
But . . . But . . . But so many of those states are in places like Oklahoma and so many of those people live in states like that and . . .

Which brings us back to knowing hay from straw. It turns out not to matter. A Heartlander will tell you that either hay *or* straw will do just fine to stuff in the mouth of a Coastal.

Quiz
ARE YOU A COASTAL OR A HEARTLANDER?

It's not *where* you live. It's *how* you live. Take this quiz to find out whether you're an Organic All-Natural Unrefined Sea Salt person or whether you're the Salt of the Earth.

Check option A or option B, then tally your scores below.

How You Eat

Option A	Option B
☐ Sushi	☐ Bait
☐ Microbrew Amber Blonde Honey Lime IPA Lager Malt Porter Stout	☐ Beer
☐ Vegan	☐ "Eat your vegetables"
☐ 9 grain bread	☐ Driveway sand
☐ "Just a salad"	☐ With a double order of fries on the side
☐ Brunch	☐ Second Breakfast
☐ Farm-to-table	☐ Farm-to–TV tray
☐ Locally sourced	☐ Microwave-to-recliner
☐ Wine flights	☐ Box of Franzia

Option A	Option B
☐ Avocado toast	☐ Bread and butter
☐ Quinoa	☐ Grits
☐ BPA-free water bottle	☐ Garden hose
☐ Stone-ground whole wheat crackers	☐ Chicken in a Biskit
☐ Whole Foods	☐ Half of a Black Angus in the freezer

How You Grew Up

Option A	Option B
☐ Playdate	☐ "Go play outside, it's only raining a little."
☐ Trophy for showing up	☐ "Next year try catching the ball."
☐ Elite preschool	☐ Finger painting with old house paint found in the garage
☐ Computer camp, art camp, theater camp, STEM camp	☐ Mowing the lawn
☐ SAT test-prep tutor	☐ Homework
☐ Unpaid internship	☐ Summer job

Option A	Option B
☐ Gap year	☐ Flunked out
☐ Backyard chickens	☐ Backyard chickens, pigs, deer, turkey, squirrels, kids, dogs, rabbits, and baby raccoon abandoned by its mother
☐ Flying to Paris for the weekend	☐ Road trip to Paris, Texas

How You See the World

Option A	Option B
☐ Personal journey	☐ RV
☐ Follow your bliss	☐ Garmin DriveLuxe 51 LMT-S GPS got a good review in *Consumer Reports*
☐ Growing as a person	☐ The dry cleaner shrank these pants
☐ "Woke"	☐ Snooze button
☐ Burning Man	☐ Out of charcoal lighter and Dad used gasoline
☐ TED Talk	☐ Brother-in-law Ted never shuts up

Option A	Option B
☐ #MeToo	☐ Smith & Wesson Airweight .38 Special in purse
☐ Prius	☐ Jumper cables
☐ Uber	☐ AAA
☐ Barista	☐ Graduate degree in philosophy
☐ Tattoo body art to express your passion	☐ Semper fi
☐ Looking for the meaning of life	☐ Looking for the TV remote
☐ Yoga	☐ Church
☐ Downward dog	☐ Remembering to feed the dog
☐ Carved stone Buddha	☐ Cast concrete Virgin Mary
☐ Climate awareness	☐ Weather report
☐ Microaggression	☐ Kick in the shin
☐ *Fearless Girl*	☐ Golda Meir, Margaret Thatcher, Corazon Aquino, Queen Elizabeth I, Joan of Arc . . .

Option A	Option B
☐ PETA	☐ Petco
☐ Social justice	☐ Judge Judy
☐ Gender fluid	☐ Tyler Perry in *Madea on the Run*
☐ Speaking truth to power	☐ Yelling at the television
☐ Room service	☐ Vending machine next to the motel ice chest
☐ Spanx	☐ Girdle
☐ CrossFit	☐ Cutting, splitting, and stacking cordwood
☐ Dry gardening with drought-resistant native species	☐ Forgetting to water the plants

RESULTS

If you checked fifteen or more items in the Option A column you're a Coastal. If you think books that have personal profile quizzes in them are a stupid waste of time you're a Heartlander.

Goodbye to
Classical Liberalism . . .

"It's the End of the World!"

People are always saying this. Especially people my age. Marcus Tullius Cicero, born in 106 B.C. and even older than I am, is famous for his apocalyptic declaration, *"O tempora! O mores!"* ("Oh, what times! Oh, what behavior!") The trouble is, sometimes Cicero and I are right.

Cicero, the greatest orator of the Roman Republic, was denouncing the political conspirator Catiline.

Catiline was a "reformer" who ran for the Roman consulship on a platform—this will sound familiar—of increased benefits for disadvantaged plebeians and *tabulae novae* ("clean slates") universal debt cancellation. Then, when he lost the election, he tried to overthrow the Roman government.

Catiline was the SPQR Bernie Sanders. Except, as a social justice warrior, Catiline actually *was* a warrior and his army of supporters really *were* armed—with swords instead of bongs, Hacky Sacks, and $5 campaign contributions.

Rome's legions killed Catiline in 62 B.C. But the Catiline conspiracy was just one episode in a long stretch

of Roman political polarization and vicious partisan in-
fighting that resulted, in 44 B.C., in Julius Caesar being
made dictator for life.

Which didn't last long. Caesar was assassinated the
next month. Nevertheless Cicero was correct in his analysis (and also dead in 43 B.C. by order of Augustus, the
next Caesar). After almost five hundred years that was
the end of the world for the Roman Republic.

And this is the end of the world for Classical Liberalism.

Civil liberties. Free speech. Property rights. Rule of
law. Representative democracy. Free enterprise. Free
trade. These are the ideas of Classical Liberalism. Since
1776 the fortunate among us have been living in places
where those ideas were embraced.

Sometimes it's been an awkward embrace. We've
watched Classical Liberalism get a clumsy "Joe Biden hug"
from advocates for greater political interference in private
life. In the matter of Classical Liberalism, "populists" want
the "classical" to be more Pop, and "liberals" want the
"liberal" to dispense largess with greater liberality.

But the core ideas persisted. And they produced excellent results. In the middle of the twentieth century
fascism was defeated and its totalitarian sister ideology
communism was contained by Classical Liberalism.

Classical liberals caused "imperialism" to be booed
off the world stage—reduced to making guest appear-
ances in the prattle of poly-sci-class academic phonies.

Classical liberals changed "colonialism" from an international villainy into an international tourist destina-
tion like the British Virgin Islands.

In the 1980s the tower of human misery constructed by the communists fell on its architects. Lenin, Stalin, Mao, and Pol Pot joined Hitler, Mussolini, and Tojo in the collapsed basement of hell.

The personal freedoms embodied in Classical Liberalism went a long way toward destroying other theoretical justifications for oppression such as antidisestablishmentarian theocracy, *Plessy v. Ferguson* segregation, and apartheid in its various forms around the world.

Given a chance, Classical Liberalism could even banish—or at least mitigate—prejudice and bigotry. Liberty means free and responsible individuals. Free and responsible individuals have a lot to do, exercising their freedoms and shouldering their responsibilities. No set of principles, however noble, can prevent people from detesting each other, but Classical Liberalism can keep people otherwise occupied and busy.

An example from the 1960s. During the height of the civil rights struggle Atlanta's sort of but not really pro-integration mayor Ivan Allen came up with a weasel-phrase slogan to indicate that the local white establishment, although not fully reconciled to civil liberties and equality before the law, was willing to—as we'd call it these days—move on. "Atlanta, a City Too Busy to Hate."

We *would* hate but we're just *so busy!*

Under the aegis of Classical Liberalism earth thrived. Global per capita GDP went, in inflation-adjusted dollars, from $3,900 in 1950 to $17,300 in 2017. Thank you, civil liberties, free speech, property rights, rule of law, representative democracy, free enterprise, and free trade.

As the tenets of Classical Liberalism spread, the governmental practice of oppression seemed to be fading.

In 1945 only the lucky few could be called citizens of a free country. Today, 39 percent of the world's population has political freedom, another 24 percent has partial freedom, and 74 percent of the world's 195 nations are at least free enough to give Classical Liberalism a try.

So says Freedom House, the nonpartisan advocacy organization for democracy, which is so nonpartisan that it was founded in 1941 by defeated presidential candidate Wendell Willkie *and* Eleanor Roosevelt. (Such, at one time, were the powers of faith in Classical Liberalism. Imagine, today, an advocacy organization founded by Hillary Clinton *and* Melania Trump.)

Classical Liberalism has had a good run. Now it's about to get run over by a bus full of stupid "post-capitalist" political trends—the new socialism, the new nationalism, the new trade war mercantilism, and the new social media platforms that drive this bus.

Vladimir Putin, Xi Jinping, Donald Trump, and the numerous candidates who ran for the 2020 Democratic presidential nomination are all onboard. So are the Brexiteers and so, for that matter, are the maniacally microregulating bureaucrats of the EU that the Brexiteers want to leave.

Wave goodbye to Classical Liberalism. Or you could just wave at the camera you're facing on your phone or computer. Too late to put a sticky note over it. Your civil liberties are already gone. Not a click falls on a keypad nor a finger taps a touch screen without the Internet seeing.

You are a fly caught in the World Wide Web. Email is blackmail with a .com on the end. Civil liberties—and the free will needed to exercise them—are impossible when someone knows *everything* about you. And someone does. Probably it's just that twerp Mark Zuckerberg who's got your every word, worry, action, attraction, emotion, motion, and notion stored in the Cloud. But how long before a more serious person or thing hacks in and starts running your life? (Jared Kushner, Greta Thunberg, George Soros, NSA, the UN, Proud Boys, IRS, NRA—you can bet that the person or thing that keeps you up at night will be what hacks you.)

And how do you know they haven't done it already? How hard can it be? The Internet treats user privacy with the same respect that snakes get in a cage at a carnival sideshow. And Zuckerberg is a thirty-five-year-old still wearing his underwear in public. His mother no doubt writes his password on the waistband of his Y-fronts with a laundry pen.

Plus the average cost of an Internet connection in the United States is $67.17 a month, so free speech isn't free anymore anyway.

Property rights will be next to go. Here too the Internet aids and abets, particularly in the destruction of intellectual property rights. Take it from me, a print journalist. "Content Is Free"—that's the founding concept of the Internet. I spent forty years as a print journalist. Now I'm a "content provider." And . . . *Content Is Free.*

Our remaining property rights, our rights to physical property, will be sacrificed either to the campaign for income equality or to the campaign against climate change (or, should these hysterias fail, to the campaign against something terrible we haven't imagined yet).

Whether property is swiped in the name of economic fairness or in the name of nature being treated unfairly will depend on which end of the world comes first: everybody on earth in bankruptcy court (total global debt is now $244 trillion, three times the size of the world economy) or everybody on earth crammed into the last 1,878 vertical feet of Mount Everest because of the rising sea level.

In the former case, a horde of people will show up at polling places under the impression that voting machines are like the slots at Mohegan Sun. If they pull the lever often enough there will be a huge payout.

The Internet tells me (for free) that, using the broadest definition of "money" (cash plus all banking and money market account balances), there's about $80 trillion in the world. The world's population is 7.5 billion. Dividing it equally, we each get $10,666.67.

We'll blow through that pretty fast, and the aftermath will be interesting. I'd make a personal recommendation about what to do in this situation, but the Second Amendment is just one more property right soon to be dispensed with.

In the climate change end-of-the-world scenario we'll all die, which makes abiding by the principles of Classical Liberalism particularly difficult. But before we die we'll panic.

I understand why people are bothered by climate change. It bothers me four times a year—arthritic winter, allergic spring, summertime bedroom A/C window unit falling out and smashing the patio furniture, and my Harris Tweed sport coat full of moth holes in the fall. But we've let our annoyance and worry be turned into abject fear. I'm sure our earthly home could use some tidying, climatologically. But when the house is a mess you get out the mop and the broom, you don't call the police.

In our panic we'll demand strict government regulation to prevent carbon emissions. And most carbon emissions result from the exercise of property rights.

Among the properties that belong to you are a pair of lungs. The Internet tells me (for free again) that those lungs emit 2.3 pounds of carbon dioxide a day. Multiply by world population and that's 17.25 trillion pounds of carbon dioxide, which is much more than the 209 billion pounds of carbon dioxide that burning fossil fuels emits daily.

You can see where the regulatory direction is headed. Exhaling to be allowed by licensed permit only and deep sighs forbidden under any circumstances. And, speaking of *exercising* your property rights, the lungs of long-distance joggers, gym rats, hot yoga practitioners, and others who engage in vigorous physical activity can emit as much as eight times the average amount of CO_2. The police would run you down, except that would cause even more global warming, so they'll shoot you from a distance.

(Yes, yes, I know. The *experts* try to explain to me that breathing isn't like burning fossil fuels because breathing doesn't involve "sequestered carbon." But I'm as dumb as the next voter and don't know sequester from Ryan Seacrest. Or, anyway, I'm as dumb as Senator Elizabeth Warren who, when she introduces a federal law against breathing, will tell us that only the rich will have to hold their breath.)

Your possessions will go away. And, because "possession is nine-tenths of the law," rule of law goes with them. (That "nine-tenths" adage isn't about squatters' rights or who's borrowed the car. It's an old maxim of English common law, first cited in print in the late sixteenth century by Richard Carew, high sheriff of Cornwall. Carew was pointing out that the main purpose of law is to protect property. Foremost in the law's protection is that property most precious to you—*you*. The foundational property right is your ownership of yourself as a free person. Much as we may hate the private islands, Park Avenue penthouses, trust funds, Learjets, limousines, and other property accumulated by the filthy rich, without property there is no freedom.

If rule of law goes away so does representative democracy—the legal system of checks and balances that's entrusted with both guidance by majorities and protection of individuals. When government takes ownership of everything the result is either the terror of collectivism or the horror of crony capitalism or, as in China, both. The checks bounce and the balances are weighted by the thumbs of special interests.

Also, lacking civil liberties and property rights, representative democracy is left with nothing to represent except the will of the mob or—as it's called these days—"activism."

We already live in a country where activists are snatching the role once played by duly elected and duly appointed officials.

When Dr. Frankenstein is up to something in his castle, does modern America send the county building inspector to check if the electrical wiring is safe? Not when a large group of activists with pitchforks and torches are available to chase Dr. Frankenstein back to the local urgent care facility and make him provide Medicare for All.

As I mentioned before, the collapse of Classical Liberalism is by no means just an American problem. The same Freedom House that brought us the good news about the growth of democracy since World War II brings us bad news in its most recent report, "Freedom in the World 2018."

- **Democracy faced its most serious crisis in decades** . . . as its basic tenets—including guarantees of free and fair elections, the rights of minorities, freedom of the press, and the rule of law—came under attack around the world.

- Seventy-one countries suffered net declines in political rights and civil liberties, with only 35 registering gains. This marked the 12th consecutive year of decline in global freedom.

And how will the end of the Classical Liberal world affect your daily life?

Imagine even a trip to the grocery store without Classical Liberalism. How about Mexican tonight? (Or is cultural appropriation forbidden now?) But, first, you need civil liberties just to leave your house. And no matter what you think about immigration, if Hispanic Americans didn't have civil liberties you wouldn't know *mierda* about Mexican food. You'd be making tacos by rolling liverwurst in Aunt Jemima pancakes and seasoning it with pumpkin pie spice. The grocery store requires free speech to advertise its specials. You could be paying twice as much for the corn tortillas as you would have paid at the other grocery store down the road. Except, without property rights, there might not be another grocery store down the road. In fact there might not be any grocery stores at all. You'll have to wait for dinner until there's a government taco handout. Furthermore, absent rule of law, just how old *is* that guacamole? And lastly, although you might not think representative democracy would come into play at the checkout counter, what if a certain kind of doofus becomes America's Augustus Caesar and the kid who's bagging your groceries double bags the Dos Equis six-pack and gets—as they call it these days—canceled for not sequestering your carbon?

O tempora! O mores!

Big Fat Politics

At the beginning of 2019 we had a thirty-five-day "government shutdown." For those with more or less libertarian views (myself included) this was a be-careful-what-you-wish-for moment.

Not that it didn't seem like a perfectly good time to shut the government down, what with the ongoing political bumfuzzlement—bum in the White House and fuzzlement in Congress.

But what I personally had in mind was more like senators and representatives going to payday lenders, cabinet members sleeping under bridges, and the president of the United States selling his wife's Manolo Blahniks on Shopify to pay the pizza delivery boy at state dinners.

Instead we got very crabby unpaid TSA agents who would have strip-searched me right in the middle of Dulles Airport if there hadn't been a long line of people at the security checkpoint begging not to see me naked.

We got Yellowstone Park rangers pawning the bears to make car payments. National Gallery curators chalking pictures on the sidewalk hoping someone would drop a quarter in their hat. And grade school field trips where the closest the kids came to a tour of the Capitol building was looking at a picture of it on the back of the $50 bills that lobbyists charge per minute.

Because the *lobbyists* weren't closed for business. And neither was any other high muck-a-muck, big noise, or Chief Itch-and-Rub in Washington. Government shut-down? Our government is so bad at everything that it can't even do nothing right.

And how did our government get so bad? Bad politics. But how did our politics get so bad? Politics grew worse because politics grew.

Sometimes when things grow it's good—when the grown kids finally move out of the house. But sometimes when things grow it's a *growth*. It's a tumor. We have a gigantic political tumor. I'm not optimistic about the biopsy.

Here I enter a definitional quagmire, and excuse me while I drag you along. The growth of politics is not the same as the growth of government. Our government is a bit of a wide load and a pie wagon and giving it the Peloton Wife treatment would be a good idea. On the other hand, there are about 330 million of us in a coun-try with a $19 trillion GDP. As to bulk, our government will always be more defensive tackle than bag of bones special-teams player kicking punts.

And government being bad is not so bad as politics being bad. In fact, our government isn't as bad as I say it is. It's just a human institution, with all the human failings that entails. (I say it's bad because I'm a political pundit, with all the human failings *that* entails.) Our government is probably as good—maybe better—than any other human institution its size. Although there are no other human institutions its size. China's equivalent to the U.S. federal budget is only slightly more than half of ours. And, much as I dislike Trump, I wouldn't trade him for Xi Jinping. (Not even if I lived in Miami and the Chinese threw in the really good defensive tackle that the Dolphins need.)

Government and politics are different. Government is . . . words fail me . . . government. Politics is the fight over who runs the government. And the fix is in because, as you may have noticed, every time politicians stage that fight a politician wins.

The growth of politics is the opposite of the growth of liberty. When liberty grows we get increased individual enterprise and expansion of free markets. We create more goods, services, and benefits to society. The pie gets bigger.

But politics is not about creating more goods, services, and benefits to society. Politics is about dividing them up.

Politics is about promising things to people. "The auction of goods about to be stolen," as H. L. Mencken put it.

The promises are lies, of course. But it isn't just the qualitative untruth of a lie that matters. The quantitative untruth matters too. When politics is a minor contest, a backyard tussle, it promises a few things to a few people. Naturally they're disappointed. But it's just a few people, a trifling number of beggars with "will vote for food" signs squatting at the polls looking for political handouts (and batting each other over the head with their pieces of cardboard). If they get a cup of joe when they thought they were going to get a chicken dinner, no big deal. (Or "New Deal." Or "Fair Deal." Or "Great Society.")

We survived those growths in the size of politics. But politics had just begun to go Baconator. Now politics is at the point of promising everything to everybody.

And everybody is disappointed. Everybody goes away empty-handed. Everybody feels cheated.

Does this make us mad at our politicians? Yes. But mostly it makes us mad at each other, because politics is a zero-sum game the way freedom and free markets are not. Zero-sum games are not played for kicks and giggles. Zero-sum games are blood sports.

Yes, there's competition in free markets. That's what makes them work. Competition is the vermouth in the martini. But as it is with martinis, so it is with free markets. For every one part competition vermouth there are six parts of that top-shelf gin called spontaneous cooperation among free people. (Which always seems to leave politicians "shaken, not stirred.")

Adam Smith pointed it out, 244 years ago. Among free people, in a free market exchange of goods and services, everyone comes out ahead. Each person gives something he or she values less in return for something he or she values more. Both sides win. I've got the Grey Goose. You've got the Noilly Prat, the olives, and the crushed ice. Bottoms up!

But in politics only one side can win. What's at stake in politics isn't goods and services, it's power. Power is always zero-sum. When I sell you goods and services I gain something in return. When I sell you power over myself—and that's the political exchange—I stand to lose everything.

Under the condition of liberty, if you have a swimming pool and a Bentley I can get a swimming pool and a Bentley too. Under the condition of politics, you can drown me in your swimming pool and run me over with your Bentley.

In politics only one side can win. Which is bad. But what's worse is this means there have to *be* sides. Faction—angry partisan faction—isn't a by-product of politics, it *is* politics. Politics cannot exist without faction. Politics cannot exist without people fighting each other. Put down the free market goods and services pie. Pick up the pie knife of politics.

Freedom brings us all together in the marketplace (although admittedly in a sometimes grumpy way when we see the cash register total). But politics carves us up. Politics pits us against each other. Politics turns us into warring tribes.

Politics hands us the spear of outrage at the slightest perceived slight to our primitive political clan, smears us with the war paint of identity politics, gives us the shield of political correctness, and tells us that we're not naked savages squatting around a smoldering fire of resentment and envy but noble Social Justice Warriors.

Politics pits one ethnic group against another. And it does it for free. It doesn't even charge us the way 23andMe or Ancestry.com do.

Politics pits men against women—as if we didn't have the institution of marriage doing a fine job of that already.

Politics pits immigrants against . . . Against *whom*? We're all immigrants. Even Native Americans just got here from the old country, twenty or thirty thousand years ago, which is about a minute before last call on the human migration clock. There'd been people in Africa for a million years.

Finally—and most dangerously—politics pits one generation of Americans against another. The millennials are mad at the baby boomers for soaking up all the Social Security and Medicare gravy while, at the same time, refusing to retire, leaving the millennials to work in a "gig economy" where they make a living by driving each other around for Uber.

There are now more millennial voters than there are OK boomers. And they've got Uber to take them to the polls while I'm still trying to figure out how that app works and whether I should get into a car driven by someone who braids her beard.

The younger generation is attracted to an expansion of politics. Partly this is because so many politicians have worked so hard to be assholes, and they obviously need to be politically defeated. But also this is because other politicians have worked so hard to convince millennials that life, like politics, is a zero-sum game. Millennials can't get *more* unless they use an expansion of politics ("socialism") to take *more away from* . . . if book-sales demographics are anything to go by . . . everybody reading this.

And politics is attracted to an expansion of politics. Indeed, politics, by its own internal logic, is driven to expand. Yet politics fails *because* it expands.

Politics is like a balloon. Or, rather, it's like a rolled-up and inflatable latex item all sixteen-year-old boys of my era carried in our wallets (more in hope than in expectation).

Politics at that scale can be a kind of "useful safe-guard to liberty." Even then it doesn't always prove reliable. A hasty wedding just before high school graduation may ensue.

But, make like a politician instead of a Romeo, and blow a lot of hot air into that inflatable latex item, it gets more fragile yet.

Actually, with politics, it's worse than the fragility that spawns the occasional bastard. The expansion of politics is hubris, and hence tragic. To overinflate politics is to start out with a Trojan, safe and secure in a little foil pack of constitutionalism, and wind up with the Hindenburg. "Oh the humanity!"

Socialism? It's not a form of government. In a free country, government may—to a greater or lesser degree—tax, spend, administrate, regulate, provide benefits, and impose stipulations, according to the will of the governed, under the rule of law. Socialism is a law unto itself. Socialism is the politicization of everything. Socialism is when the stakes in the political battle are so high that they include control of the entire socioeconomic system. In this kind of boxing match it's the referee—the sovereign people of the United States—who's down for the count.

Socialism has been tried. And tried. We have a proven track record of how it goes. A track record that's more than a century long as of the October 2017 one hundredth anniversary of the Russian Revolution. *That* went well.

So how is it that so many young, fresh, new voters and so many politicians—not so young but full of fresh, new ambition—are suddenly in love with socialism and unworried about its consequences?

Ed Crane, founder of the libertarian think tank the Cato Institute, emailed me a joke swiped from the Internet that explains it as well as anything does.

A libertarian walks into a bar at 9:58 p.m., and happens to sit down on a bar stool next to Alexandria Ocasio-Cortez. The libertarian stares up at the bar's TV screen as the 10 o'clock news comes on. The news crew has its camera on a man standing on a ledge of a tall building, getting ready to jump.

Alexandria looks at the libertarian and says, "Do you think he'll jump?"

The libertarian says, "I bet he will."

Alexandria says, "Well, I bet he won't."

The libertarian puts $20 on the bar and says, "You're on."

Just as Alexandria puts her own money on the bar the man on the TV screen jumps off the ledge and falls to his death. Alexandria is very upset but she hands her $20 to the libertarian, saying, "Okay, here's your money."

The libertarian says, "I can't take your money. I saw this earlier on the five o'clock news, and I knew he would jump."

Alexandria says, "I saw it too. *But I didn't think he'd do it again.*"

But Thank You Anyway, Partisan Politicans

There is an oft-cited apothegm credited to the Spanish mystic and Carmelite nun St. Teresa of Avila (1515–82): "There are more tears shed over answered prayers than over unanswered prayers."

Likewise—let us hope to heaven—there are more smiles spread by things that we had prayed would never happen.

And certainly, if we're people of conscience and faith, we prayed that American politics wouldn't become as bad as they are at the moment.

But bad politics do have a few good aspects. (Or such is my fervent wish in this otherwise bleak political season.)

First, let us be thankful that, in our domestic politics, we are a bitterly divided nation. This sounds like an oxymoronic kind of gratitude, but highly polarized partisanship about *internal* political issues is, in fact, a sort of luxury. It shows that America is blessed with not being under grave *external* threat.

When America is under grave external threat, Americans unite in a jiffy—the way we did after Pearl Harbor

or 9/11. This unity is an awesome thing to behold. Also
it's a "shock and awesome" thing to behold if you're an
enemy of America. If you're someone who's caused the
grave external threat we're going to come and get you
whether you're in Berlin, Tokyo, Abbottabad, or a hole
in the ground in Idlib, Syria.

But when America is *not* under grave external threat,
we Americans can go back to our tradition of indulging
ourselves in a wild extravagance of bickering with each
other, the way we've been doing since 1776.

Of course these internal political contretemps can get
out of hand. The Civil War comes to mind. However, as
heated as America's arguments may be at the moment,
2020 is not 1861. Fort Sumter is not taking any incom-
ing. Our political battles are all smoke and no lethal fire.

(Except from a few fringe lunatics, of course. But
we've always had those. President James A. Garfield, a
chief executive who was unpolarizing to the point of
complete obscurity, was assassinated by one. The killer
was Charles Guiteau, who must have been some kind
of nut even to have known that James A. Garfield was
president.)

These days our weapons are just TV shows and other
such media pie fights and the cannonballs don't land
with lethal effect, they land with stupid splats like Sean
Hannity and Rachel Maddow.

A second thing to be thankful for is how bad politics
are a healthy reminder that politics *are* bad. Being a
"good" politician actually, specifically, requires committing every single one of the Seven Deadly Sins.

Pride foremost, naturally. What kind of too-big-for-your-britches swell-headed grandstander has the flash-the-brass conceit to come right out and claim that he or she ought to be president of the United States? Let alone is capable of the task? It's a nearly impossible job, and anyone who doesn't admit this is unqualified for the position. The only kind of people we should want to be president are the kind of people we'd have to drag, cursing and kicking, into the Oval Office. (Anyone know Clint Eastwood's current whereabouts?)

Envy is pride's inevitable twin. Even the most successful politician is always envious of someone whose britches are more widely split at the seams, whose head has a more pronounced case of mumps above the ears, whose bleachers are jammed with a larger crowd of ripe sucks. Hillary Clinton's green glow of envy still shines so brightly that you can use it to read newspaper stories about Donald Trump at midnight across the street from her house in Chappaqua.

Wrath is the defining emotion of politics today. All the participants, elected and electorate alike, are furiously shouting at each other.

It's like the time that a bunch of Boston Irish, down in Southie, decided to start a rowing club to compete with the Ivy League.

The Irishmen were big, strong men, and they practiced hard every day, but they kept losing. They lost to Yale. They lost to Princeton. They lost to Dartmouth.

Finally the Irish team captain says, "Sure and the Harvard rowing team's been winning all year. Seamus, you go sneak over to Cambridge there and hide in the bushes by the Harvard boathouse and see how it is that they're doing it."

So Seamus sneaks over to Cambridge and hides in the bushes by the Harvard boathouse and watches the Harvard crew team.

And Seamus comes back and he says, "Begorrah, but I think I know where we're going wrong. We're supposed to have one fellow screaming and yelling and the other eight are supposed to be rowing."

Greed, **Gluttony**, and **Lust** play vital roles in politics. And I'm not referring to money, food, and romps between the sheets. Although what with corruption, $1,000-a-plate campaign fund-raising dinners, and #MeToo stalking the halls of power, those transgressions do abound. But the true mortal sin of politics is greed, gluttony, and lust for power. The avaricious, the voracious, and the horny may be forgiven, but people whose deepest desire is to lord it over others go to hell.

And let us not forget **Sloth**. Politics might seem to be a busy and active profession with laziness rare among politicians. But politicians can be indolent, idle do-nothings when it comes to answering the needs of the American people. To give just one sinful example: The Fifteenth Amendment to the Constitution was ratified on February 3, 1870.

Section 1. The right of citizens of the United States to vote shall not be denied or abridged by the United States or by any State on account of race, color, or previous condition of servitude.

Section 2. The Congress shall have power to enforce this article by appropriate legislation.

Then came *ninety-five years* of Jim Crow state and local lawmaking until the Voting Rights Act of 1965 was passed.

Lastly, let us give thanks that our bad politics provide our terrible politicians with something relatively harmless to do. They've been spending most of the past two years campaigning on their godawful political platforms. This has kept them out of our hair and away from the rest of us in remote places like Iowa, New Hampshire, and the Twittersphere.

It could be worse. They could be engaged in ordinary day-to-day life nearby. For example, if Joe Biden hadn't been being driven from place to place on the campaign trail he might have been driving his own car in typical elderly fashion at 15 mph the wrong way down one-way streets while leaving his turn signal on for half an hour.

And anyone with any money invested in real estate can feel thankful that Donald Trump has been too busy to send more real estate development into bankruptsy.

Speaking of which, Elizabeth Warren's specialty as a law school professor was bankruptcy law. If she'd been in private practice she might have been working for

Google or Amazon or Microsoft, and Google or Amazon or Microsoft would be bankrupt.

And South Bend, Indiana, might as well be, with a poverty rate of 25.4 percent compared to the national average of 12.3 percent. Plus the city's violent crime rate is 157 percent higher than the nation's. Whatever Pete Buttigieg was doing as South Bend's mayor, South Bend residents must be thankful that he took some time off to do it to Iowans.

Let us all bow our heads in thanks for bad politics.

Robin Hood Arithmetic

W. C. *Fields* *to his adopted daughter Poppy: "I am*
like Robin Hood: I take from the rich and give to
the poor."
Poppy: *"What poor?"*
Fields: *"Us poor."*

—*Poppy* (1936)

The Sherwood Forest ethic has a long-standing appeal. The legend dates back at least to the thirteenth century. Today all politicians promise to be something of a Robin Hood and some politicians promise to be Robin, Little John, Friar Tuck, and Maid Marian rolled into one: free health care, free day care, free college tuition, forgiveness of outstanding student loans, Universal Basic Income (UBI), and throw in the kitchen sink of subsidized housing for the homeless who crowd the sidewalks of San Francisco and Portland where everybody votes for politicians who promise subsidized housing for the homeless.

Taking from the rich and giving to the poor is a not unkindly notion and often a tempting idea. Alas, some Sheriff of Nottingham math is in order.

The 10 percent of Americans who earn the most money make a total of about $4.75 trillion a year. These are the rich. Not that they're crazy rich. An annual household income of $118,000 puts people in the top 10 percent. But let's not quibble; $118,000 ain't hay. They're the rich. We'll take from them. And, what the heck, let's take *everything* from them. All $4.75 trillion.

Now let's give to the poor. Or try to. The federal budget for 2020—without any new programs for dispensing costly goods and services at no cost to the recipients— is . . . you guessed it . . . $4.75 trillion.

A 100 percent tax on the income of the rich would last the federal government one year.

Then, the next year, when the IRS comes to take 100 percent of rich people's incomes . . . My guess is they've moved to the Cayman Islands.

Even if the rich stick around, they haven't been getting any money all year so now they're the poor, and they qualify for getting all the free stuff too.

How are we going to pay for it? I suppose we could ask the 10 percent to keep working while continuing to not get paid. They might be crabby about that.

So let's not tax income. Let's tax wealth. Being bloated plutocrats isn't about what the rich *earn*, it's about what they *own*. The filthy rich still have a fortune socked away in physical assets, stocks, bonds, real estate, and the secret Cayman Islands bank accounts they all use. (Slip a little Medicare for All and UBI to Cayman Islands bank tellers and we'll have rich people's PIN numbers in no time.)

America has tremendous wealth disparity. This is obvious, although wealth disparity is somewhat harder to quantify than income disparity. People have to report their incomes. People do not have to report their Chanel bags, Hermès scarves, Prada shoes, and Versace frocks. Also the value of such luxuries—not to mention the value of stocks, bonds, and real estate—fluctuates. (And people are subject to fibbing.)

Nonetheless, a search of what statistics are available about personal wealth indicates that the net worth of U.S. households is approximately $95 trillion and that the richest 10 percent of Americans own at least 75 percent of that wealth or, in round numbers, $71 trillion.

Now we're talking real money. We'll have plenty to give to the poor—$71 trillion. Oops, make that $69.5 trillion. (We forgot to subtract $1.5 billion in outstanding student loans.)

Also, we'll have to pay off the U.S. national debt—$22 trillion. The reason we'll have to pay off the national debt is that America's top 10 percent of business owners, corporate executives, high tech savants, doctors, lawyers, and other professionals have given up on working for a living and are lazing around their beach houses (soon to be expropriated).

They're not buying any Chanel bags, Hermès scarves, Prada shoes, and Versace frocks or Tesla Model X SUVs or Bertram yachts or Sub-Zero wine refrigerators.

They've quit paying the landscaper and the pool service. They're letting the grass grow and the Jacuzzi get scummy. They've fired the nanny and aren't tipping the pizza delivery guy anymore.

This makes America's economy so lousy that nobody will ever lend the U.S. government any money ever again. And everybody who has already lent the U.S. government money is sending bill collectors dunning us to pay the money back. So we'll have to settle up the national debt—$22 trillion.

Okay, that still leaves us with $47.5 trillion to give to the poor.

But that will mean a much larger federal budget. It's estimated that Medicare for All would cost $3.2 trillion a year. And a Universal Basic Income would cost $3.8 trillion a year. (Free college tuition is just a rounding error of about $70 billion a year. We won't even count that.)

The Green New Deal is harder to price. It's more of a letter to Santa than a piece of legislation. The "I want a pony" might mean an old Shetland free from the local animal shelter. Or it might mean a racehorse sired by Northern Dancer, selling for $26 million. But Alexandria Ocasio-Cortez herself has mentioned a figure of $10 trillion over the next decade for the Green New Deal, and let's take her word for it: $1 trillion a year.

So current spending of $4.75 trillion + $3.2 trillion + $3.8 trillion + $1 trillion = almost $13 trillion.

A Robin Hood president (assuming he or she has a Maid Marian House of Representatives and a Friar Tuck Senate) will have $47.5 trillion to give to the poor. But divide $47.5 trillion by $13 trillion and we see that all the money that all the rich people have will last three years and eight months—running out right at the end of Robin Hood's four-year presidential term.

If Robin wants to get reelected, that band of Merry Men will have to invent some new kind of economic arithmetic, perhaps the kind of economic arithmetic they have in Venezuela.

On the Other Hand . . .
Just Give Them the Money

What makes people poor has been debated for centuries by scholars, moralists, theorists, policy makers, and pundits like me—a bunch of idiots engaged in a huge waste of time. What makes people poor is not having money.

According to the U.S. Census there are 38.1 million poor people in America. These people are not poor because the federal government doesn't spend money on poor people. It does.

The Congressional Research Service keeps track of these things. The CRS is a nonpartisan agency in the Library of Congress—serene and calm midst the political chaos of Washington. (Which is not so rare as one might think. Although some other nonpartisan federal agencies may be so serene and calm that they've nodded off at their desks, because the CRS figures below come with a note: "FY2016—most recent year for which federal spending data were available.")

Anyway, the CRS has a report called "Federal Spending on Benefits and Services for People with Low Income."

In the report we see that the federal government spends $877.5 billion annually on these benefits and services. And let us note that this spending does *not* include Social Security, Medicare, unemployment insurance, or Affordable Care Act subsidies.

However, the $877.5 billion does include $467.8 billion spent on health care for the poor in programs such as Medicaid. Working on the assumption that 38.1 million poor people is bad enough, and that we don't want them to be poor *and* sick, let's not count health care costs as "benefits and services." Let's just call it common human decency.

Subtracting $467.8 billion from $877.5 billion leaves us with $409.7 billion. This is still a lot of money. Why does spending it on poor people seem to be so ineffective at eliminating poverty?

Maybe the answer is to be found, of all places, on the Republican House Budget Committee website, where the following statement appears:

> There are at least 92 federal programs designed to help lower-income Americans. For instance, there are dozens of education and job-training programs, 17 different food-aid programs, and over 20 housing programs.

Many people may think that Republicans don't want to "help lower-income Americans." I feel that's harsh. But, for the sake of argument, let's *stipulate* that Republicans don't want to help. What interests me about their statement is not its implicit criticism of federal poverty program surfeit (explicit criticism follows). What interests me is the phrase, with italics added, "There are *at least* 92 federal programs . . ."

These are *Republicans*! We've just said—for the sake of argument—that they deplore poverty programs, that they want to get rid of them all. You'd think they'd be keeping careful track of each and every poverty program they want to eliminate. Yet even Republicans don't know how many of these programs exist. Nobody does.

Just give poor people the money.

Divide $409.7 billion by 38.1 million and each poor person gets $10,753.28 a year. It's not any more than we're spending now. And it's not like it's going to make them stinking rich. The U.S. Department of Health and Human Services puts the poverty line for an individual at $12,490 a year.

But there's no law against poor people having a friend (although there may be some rule against it in one of the 92+ federal programs). And the HHS poverty line for a household of two is $16,910.

Buddy up and you get $21,507. And a household of four—current poverty line $25,750—gets $43,013.

Just give them the money.

No, I don't know exactly how to do it. As a policy wonk I'm all wonk and no policy. But the government is damn efficient at taking away by means of payroll withholding, and I'm sure it can be equally efficient at handing out by payroll forthcoming. Or something like that.

Just give them the money.

It's Time to Make Rich People Uncomfortable Again

Lately there has been a lot of anger and indignation about wealth inequality. Some blame this on . . . wealth inequality. I blame it on rich people in T-shirts.

I won't mention Mark Zuckerberg by name. But, honestly, young man, you're thirty-five years old, worth $72 billion, and you're wearing what a preschooler would wear the first time he's allowed to dress himself.

Yes, I'm also going around in an untucked "My Kid Went to College and All I Got Was This Lousy . . ." But I've earned it. Or, rather, I haven't. I can't afford a Savile Row morning suit, Turnbull & Asser dress shirt, Hermès cravat, and pair of bespoke John Lobb oxfords. And— taking out the trash, gassing up the car, and ordering an Egg McMuffin at the drive-through window—I wouldn't be comfortable wearing them.

But Mark Zuckerberg in his Fruit of the Looms seems *too* comfortable. And this makes us mad.

There was a time when wealth was distributed far less equitably, but we weren't as resentful of the rich. We resented our poverty, but we were relieved that we didn't have to put on striped pants and spats to have breakfast.

Being rich looked very uncomfortable. Rich people's clothes were stiff and starchy and they wore lots of them. Rich men were choked by tall collars and pinched by high-button shoes. Rich women were corseted to the point of kidney failure, constrained in so much crinoline and brocade that they might as well have been wearing off-the-shoulder burqas, and encumbered by bustles large enough that they couldn't turn sideways without knocking over a footman and the parlor maid.

Now we have Jeff Bezos in a New Kids on the Block bomber jacket, Bill Gates outfitted in Mr. Rogers sweaters and Gloria Steinem's old aviators and cutting his own hair, Elon Musk smoking pot on TV, and Richard Branson looking like the guy at the end of the bar muttering lines from *The Big Lebowski*. That's not counting the various plutocrats caught in *Us* and the *Star* wearing nothing much at all.

If rich people start getting any more comfortable police will be shooing them off park benches.

Rich people are also having fun—flying their own rocketships, sending lewd selfies, buying private islands (Manhattan, for example). Having fun was something rich people didn't used to do, at least not as far as we poor people could tell.

They went to the opera. It was like Vaudeville except without the tap dancing, acrobatics, magic tricks, and jokes. (If opera did have jokes they were sung in a foreign language and nobody got the punch lines.)

Rich people—and there were supposedly only Four Hundred of them—gathered in Mrs. Astor's ballroom. They waltzed like sticks in the mud to music that would put the dead to sleep and ate and drank tiny things from tiny plates and glasses. They never knocked the bung out of the beer keg, danced a polka, or sang

Your baby has gone down the drain hole,
Your baby has gone down the plug,
The poor little thing was so skinny and thin
He should have been bathed in a jug!

Being rich meant living in a big drafty house with no privacy because the footman and parlor maid you clobbered with your bustle were always poking around. The rooms had odd names, such as "conservatory," "lavatory," "butler's pantry." (Was the butler in there panting? What was he up to that caused him to be short of breath?)

You had to wait to eat dinner until 8 p.m. Table manners were complicated. Which knife do you use to eat peas? And strange foods were served—terrapin soup (boiled turtle), shad roe (eggs that not only weren't fried but came from a fish), and pheasant under glass (dangerously breakable).

Rich people trying to have fun didn't look like much fun either. They got soaked in their yachts, broke their necks on their polo ponies, and wore themselves to a frazzle walking all over tarnation hitting things with a stick for no reason in a game called golf.

Even when relaxing they had to get dressed up according to strict social protocol. If you showed up to a yacht race wearing plus fours and a tam-o'-shanter Commodore Vanderbilt would dunk you.

These days rich people are behaving just like the rest of us. Or just like the rest of us would if we were rich. The trouble is we can't afford to be rich slobs the way rich slobs can. They're not satisfied with having all the money. They want all the fun too. And *that's* not fair.

Let's make rich people uncomfortable again. Maybe tax the dickens out of them. But somehow taxation never enriches *me*. Let's require everyone with a net worth over $100 million to wear a top hat at all times. This does nothing to fix income inequality but what a swell target for snowballs, brickbats, and rotten fruit.

Negative Rights vs. Positive Rights

It's Positively Confusing

There's a reason why so much political thinking starts out in the neighborhood of Idealism, crosses Naive Street, and winds up in Stupid.

The reason is confusion between "negative" rights and "positive" rights. We all agree that rights are wonderful and we've got a lot of them—at least in this country—and we should get a lot more.

But there are two kinds of rights: *Getoutta Here* Rights and *Gimmie* Rights. Or, as they're called in political theory, Negative Rights and Positive Rights.

Negative Rights are our rights to be left alone—to do, be, think, say (and buy and sell) whatever we want as long as our behavior doesn't cause real harms. (Microaggressions don't count unless you were somehow infected by a salmonella microbe in the process of being brushed off at the food co-op for not bringing your own re-usable shopping bag.)

Positive Rights are our rights to real *goods*—our right to get things. The right to education. The right to health care. The right to a living wage. Et cetera.

Negative Rights are front and center in the Constitution and the Declaration of Independence: "certain unalienable rights . . . Life, Liberty, and the Pursuit of Happiness." All ten rights in the of Bill of Rights are Negative Rights (except, maybe, the Sixth and Seventh Amendment Positive Right to a jury if you're put on trial for violating other people's Negative Rights by giving them food poisoning).

Positive Rights are front and center in political activism protests and politicians' election campaigns—"A chicken in every pot." (That was a Republican slogan in the 1928 presidential race. It would come back to peck the Republicans in 1932.)

This chicken isn't mentioned in the Constitution or the Declaration of Independence because our founding fathers—savvy political thinkers—would have asked, "Where did the chicken come from? Who did it belong to before? How did the chicken get into every pot, apparently for free, without impairing someone's right to make a living as a chicken farmer?"

Your right to do, be, think, and say in no way impinges on anyone else's right to do, be, think, or say. And, if you have even a rudimentary understanding of free market economics, you know that your right to buy and sell doesn't impinge on the buying and selling rights of others.

But your right to physical items, such as a free education, impinges on everybody. In order for you to be given a thing, that thing (or some tax-and-spend portion of it) has to be taken from somebody else. The person from whom the thing is taken loses negative rights so that you can gain positive ones.

This is not to say that Negative Rights are always wonderful or ought to be unlimited in scope. You have the right to stand on a street corner and say, "I'm a Nazi pig!" Whether you have the right to stand on a street corner and say to passersby, "*You're* a Nazi pig!" is a more complicated question. And if you stand on a street corner with a bullhorn and yell, "YOU'RE A NAZI PIG!" in the middle of the night the police should come and negate your negative right with a pair of handcuffs.

Nor are Positive Rights evil. Free public primary and secondary schools are a benefit to society. (Although vouchers for private school tuition might be more beneficial.) And I'm in favor of college degrees that are at least reasonably priced. (I got government help paying for school. And not because of academic merit. The government's attitude in my day was "America needs Mediocre Students Too.") I believe America should have a medical system that guarantees everyone treatment without going bankrupt from hospital bills. (Nobody should lose the house. The boat? Maybe. But not the house.) And decent pay for every job ($12 an hour for congressmen) is a worthy goal even if I think an expanding economy is more likely than a law to provide generous paychecks without driving people into the labor black market. (E.g., congressmen getting paid under the table—except that seems to be happening already.)

But are these Positive Rights really "rights"? It's the right question to ask. Idealists ought to ask it. They'd be better off changing their terminology. Idealism should be expressed as moral obligation not political cant. This particular respecter of Negative Rights is more likely to be moved by "Please" than "You're a Nazi pig."

When liberals, progressives, and democratic socialists quit demanding rights and begin invoking duties—our society's duty to fund education, proved health care, and pay living wages even to congressmen—then I'll start listening.

For Extra Credit:
Why Do We Call Rights
"Negative" and "Positive"?

Part of the confusion between the two types of rights comes from their bassackward names. Negative Rights produce mostly positive effects while Positive Rights can have negative consequences.

Blame the nomenclature on Russian-born philosopher, political theorist, and Oxford professor Isaiah Berlin (1909–97). He coined the terms "negative freedom" and "positive freedom" to describe how our desire to have a political system that (negatively) provides us with liberty clashes with our desire to have a political system that (positively) provides us with stuff.

Berlin was a great champion of "negative freedom" but he was not a native English-speaker.

Sympathy vs. Empathy

Is It Better To Hold People's Hands or Bust into Their Heads?

The difference between sympathy and empathy is the difference between *understanding* what others feel and *feeling* what they feel. Whether you're sympathetic or you're empathetic can make a big difference. Especially if you're neither and treat everybody like a cat treats an injured mouse. You'll end up eating cat food, emotionally speaking.

Sympathy and empathy both would seem to be good things. Modern moralizing, however, tends to favor empathy over sympathy. The sympathetic formulation "Our thoughts and prayers are with you" is mocked. More to current taste in virtue is the empathetic saying—often cited as a wise Native American aphorism—"Never judge someone until you've walked a mile in his shoes."

Yet it bears mentioning that, as the comedian Emo Philips says, "Never judge someone until you've walked a mile in his shoes. That way, when you do judge him, you're a mile away and you have his shoes."

Also, after lacing up the other person's footwear, a lot depends on where you're walking *to*. If you're walking a mile to his trailer home from his minimum-wage midnight shift job that's one thing. If you're walking a mile to the nineteenth hole across the fairways and greens of Augusta National that's another, even if the shoes pinch.

Sympathy and empathy play important roles in business and politics. And politics *is* a business. But let's delay discussing politics for a moment. Right now everybody on every side of every political issue is so pissed off that the finer emotions, such as sympathy and empathy, have been pushed into the dumpster at the trailer park or the sand trap at Augusta.

Let's first take an example from business. Facebook and Amazon present a paradigmatic contrast between sympathy and empathy.

Leaving aside Facebook's current reputational and regulatory problems and Amazon's 50 percent dominance of online commerce and much larger market capitalization, Facebook is by far the more extraordinary business success.

That's because Amazon is, with all its e-bells and e-whistles, just a store that delivers—which the corner grocery had a boy doing a hundred years ago.

Facebook came out of nowhere from nothing, a product nobody knew existed that filled no stated need or obvious want and suddenly everybody had to have it.

The idea behind Facebook was Harvard's *Face Book*, a campus publication containing the pictures and names of everyone in the Harvard dorms. Zuckerberg was immediately sympathetic to the idea that everyone would "like" to know other people.

Whether there was any empathy involved, I have no idea. Maybe Zuckerberg was lonely. Or—captain of his prep school fencing team, founding Facebook with his dormmates, member of Alfa Epsilon Pi fraternity— maybe he wasn't. But no empathy was necessary. All that was needed was *understanding* what others feel.

Amazon is different. Jeff Bezos empathized with his customers. He put himself in our place, which is sitting on our butts in front of a computer thinking, "It would be a hassle to go out and shop." Whether he has any sympathy for us, who can tell? Sympathy is beside the point.

As it is with the business of business, so it is with the business of politics. For an example here, let's cool off and go back in time to a period that we can view with relatively dispassionate eyes.

George H. W. Bush and Bill Clinton present a paradigmatic contrast between sympathy and empathy.

Bush was a deeply sympathetic man. He cared about other people's feelings. And he was no dummy. He understood why people felt the way they felt.

On the other hand, Bush never seemed to have the imagination or temperament to practice empathy—to project himself into other people's lives. In fact, George may have thought that would be rude, too intrusive, too inappropriately personal.

Meanwhile, Bill Clinton was the most inappropriately personal man on earth. He had no problem projecting himself into other people's . . . underwear. Not to mention lives.

Clinton was Mr. Empathy. "I feel your pain." And when he said that he probably—in his overimaginative theatrical brain full of shallow adolescent sensitivity— meant it. For a moment. Until it was somebody else's turn for Bill to feel their . . . whatever.

But did Bill have any sympathy for other people? We'll have to ask Hillary. You first.

Bush's calm, reasonable, and self-controlled attitude toward the mild recession at the end of his administration was interpreted as cold-hearted. His apparent lack of empathy cost him his reelection.

Clinton's ability to act the part of Empathizer in Chief won him the White House.

Yet, in retrospect, we see one of them as a kind, decent man who loved America and Americans and who did his best for his fellow citizens. And we sympathize.

And we see the other as having nothing but the most sympathetic possible feelings—for himself. Just an old, conceited, rich crony capitalist from whom nobody ever wants to hear anything again. And we don't empathize with him at all.

As emotions go, sympathy is more sympathetic than empathy. Trying to understand people's feelings is steadier, more sensible, and less self-dramatizing than trying to project oneself into their underwear or steal their shoes. Nevertheless. Empathy may be a better business tool than sympathy, as George H. W. Bush learned in his loss to Bill Clinton.

And where do you think Facebook and Amazon will be in ten years?

When I mention Facebook to my college-age daughter she doesn't just roll her eyes at me like I'm the extinct social media brontosaurus that I am. She also gives me a look of alarmed exasperation as if I'd suggested she give up Uber and start hitchhiking.

"Facebook is *creepy*," she says. "The ads stalk you. The *people* stalk you. All your data gets hacked."

As for where Amazon will be in ten years . . . Excuse me, the delivery man is at the door.

Patriotism vs. Nationalism

The difference between patriotism and nationalism is the difference between the love a father has for his family and the love a *Godfather* has for his family—the Bonanno family, the Colombo family, the Gambino family, the Genovese family, the Lucchese family . . .

Patriotism is a warm and personal business. Nationalism is another business entirely, the kind of business Tessio talks to Tom Hagen about after Tessio's betrayal of Michael Corleone.

Tessio: "Tell Mike it was just business."

In 1945 George Orwell wrote an essay, "Notes on Nationalism," for the British magazine *Polemic*. The essay is long and too detailed in its analysis of Nazi, Stalinist, and Trotskyite political ideas that were put out with the trash long ago (although sometimes, unfortunately, recycled). But—in severe condensation—what Orwell has to say is:

Nationalism is not to be confused with patriotism . . . By "patriotism" I mean devotion to a particular

place and a particular way of life, which one believes
to be the best in the world but has no wish to force
on other people . . . Nationalism, on the other hand,
is inseparable from the desire for power. The abiding purpose of every nationalist is to secure more
power and prestige, *not* for himself but for the nation or other [ideological, theological, ethnic, racial,
etc.] unit in which he has chosen to sink his own
individuality.

Sinking your own individuality into anything is not
a prescription for happiness. Even if what you're sinking
it into is beer. Maybe especially if it's beer. But being a
White Nationalist—or Black Nationalist or Hindu Nationalist or Islamic Nationalist or Gay Nationalist or
Whatever Nationalist—is worse than being drunk.

At least if you're drunk you're not part of a mass
movement. (Although I have seen something close to
the sinking of individuality into a menacing unit at
O'Rourke family Irish wakes. But too many O'Rourkes
fall down or pass out, so it ends up being more mass
than movement. Also, we have to sober up and go to
Mass the next day.)

What makes the units that comprise mass movements
worrisome is just what Orwell points out. You lose your
individuality. When you lose your individuality, other
people—who aren't part of your mass movement, who
aren't nationalists in your "nation"—lose their individuality to you. They cease to be people and become "other
people."

You don't see these Others as individuals, and it becomes easy to be afraid of them, hate them, regard them in a jealous way, and want to exert power over them.

As Orwell goes on to say:

> As soon as fear, hatred, jealousy and power worship are involved, the sense of reality becomes unhinged . . . the sense of right and wrong becomes unhinged also. There is no crime, absolutely none, that cannot be condoned when "our" side commits it . . . one cannot *feel* that it is wrong, Loyalty is involved, and so pity ceases to function.

Nationalism turns people into assholes or—as they're called everywhere in America except the part of New England where I live—Patriots fans.

Yes, we call ourselves "Patriots," but everybody knows we're really "Patriot Nation." It's Chicago Cubs fans who are patriotic.

Cubs fan: "I hope our team beats all the other teams."

Patriots fan: "*What* other teams? There *aren't* any other teams. And if there are any other teams I hope they die in a plane crash!"

I am myself a native patriotic Ohioan—"Round on the Ends and 'HI' in the Middle!" I am devoted to that particular place and to the Ohio way of life, which I believe to be the best in the world.

But I have no wish to force other people to go on family vacations to the birthplaces of all seven U.S. presidents who were born in Ohio (William Henry Harrison, Ulysses Grant, Rutherford Hayes, James Garfield, Benjamin Harrison, William McKinley, William Taft, and Warren Harding), eat salads with miniature marshmallows in them, mist up when they hear Chrissie Hynde sing "My City Was Gone," argue about whether *WKRP in Cincinnati* or *The Drew Carey Show* was the best TV program ever, and get suicidal if something goes wrong in "The Game" and Michigan beats Ohio State.

I don't want Ohio to conquer the world, or even Michigan. I don't want everyone in the world to become an Ohioan. We'd run out of miniature marshmallows. And, come to that, I haven't personally lived in Ohio for almost fifty years. But I'm still a loyal Buckeye.

Reading further in Orwell's essay I discover, to my surprise, that the way I feel about Ohio means I'm making a moral effort.

> Nationalistic loves and hatreds . . . are part of the make-up of most of us, whether we like it or not. Whether it is possible to get rid of them I do not know, but I do believe that it's possible to struggle against them, and that this is essentially a *moral* effort. It is a question first of all of discovering what one really is, what one's feelings really are, and then of making allowance for the inevitable bias [Boo, Wolverines!] . . . The emotional urges which are inescapable . . . should be able to exist side by side with an

acceptance of reality. [Okay, okay, Tom Brady played for Michigan.] But this, I repeat, needs a *moral* effort.

So become a patriot and you, too, like me, can turn into a more moral person than Michael Corleone turned into—not to mention those fearful, hateful, jealous, power-hungry people who root for Michigan.

Big Brother (*and* Everyone Else)
Is Watching You

Thoughts on Rereading 1984

I confess that until recently I'd given George Orwell's *1984* short shrift in my personal memory hole of frightening books. "Yeah, yeah," I thought, "a 'telescreen' that watches you while you watch it. Big deal. It's called a pop-up ad." And I thought, "At least Winston Smith can smoke anywhere he wants."

I'd forgotten what a powerful, terrifying, and tragic novel *1984* is. I forgot because I had read the book a couple of times and was under the impression that I understood it.

1984 tells the story of a totalitarianism so total that it's not satisfied with eliminating Smith, a decent, conscientious individual, but must eliminate his decency, his conscience, and his individuality before it kills him.

When I read *1984* in high school I thought, "This is what the commies are doing in the Soviet Union."

When I read *1984* in college I thought, "This is what the Man is doing in AmeriKKKa."

But when I read it as a mature (that is to say, old and worried) adult I was shocked. I realized, "This is what we're doing to *ourselves!*"

In *1984* Winston Smith *can't* turn off the spying, intrusive telescreen. Our situation is much worse. Winston had only one telescreen. We have dozens of the things—desktops, laptops, iPads, iPhones, game boxes. And we, of our own free will, *refuse* to turn them off.

We don't live in Winston Smith's horrible world—yet. But we seem to be doing everything that Orwell foresaw to create that world.

Everything and more. The nation of Oceania where Winston lives is a one-party state like Nazi Germany or the U.S.S.R. We've topped that. We've got *two* parties in our one-party state.

Both the "progressive" Democrats and the "conservative" Republicans are intent on making *1984* come true.

The LeftRight Party is the party that rules America. Members of the LeftRight Party practice the doublethink that Big Brother demands in *1984.* As Orwell explains it, doublethink is "to hold simultaneously two opinions which canceled out, knowing them to be contradictory and believing in both of them." (Ask former Attorney General Jeff Sessions about the dueling Republican/ Democratic House Intelligence Committee memos on the Mueller Russia probe.)

Orwell captures totalitarianism's interference in every aspect of existence in the first sentence of his book: ". . . the clocks were striking thirteen." Whenever the authorities start meddling with ancient and customary traditions something is wrong. So it was when President Jimmy Carter tried to put America on the metric system. And so it is today with an ancient and customary tradition we used to have, that the president of the United States was someone you would welcome into your home.

1984 has a "Two Minute Hate" where everyone has to stop what they're doing and despise Emmanuel Goldstein, "Enemy of the People." We voluntarily stop what we're doing and spend lots more than two minutes despising Donald Trump on MSNBC. Or, if that doesn't suit us, we despise Nancy Pelosi for hours on Fox News.

Winston Smith "set his features into the expression of quiet optimism which it was advisable to wear when facing the telescreen." This is nothing compared to the expression of smug and idiotic blowhard certainty that it is advisable to wear when facing the cameras on MSNBC or Fox.

Winston works in the Ministry of Truth, where his job is to rewrite history. He obeys the party slogan, "Who controls the past controls the future: who controls the present controls the past." Some LeftRight Party members tear down monuments to Civil War soldiers who died bravely having no idea they were wrong, while other LeftRight Party members dress in red baseball caps that declare they'll make America what it always has been.

In *1984* a language, Newspeak, has been invented to replace English. The purpose of Newspeak is "to limit the range of thought" by removing all previous mental associations and nuances of meaning from the vocabulary. The people of Oceania will be forced to use this language. Members of the LeftRight Party have been much more creative. They've invented not one but several languages that limit the range of thought. And they have gotten people to speak those languages without using force. Thus no one is crippled or blind or deaf anymore, much less a moron. They are all "differently abled." And no one even tries to discover the truth because the "lamestream media" is full of "fake news."

Orwell has a party member say, "Orthodoxy means not thinking." Members of our conjoined twin LeftRight Party aren't thinking *twice as much*.

"The heresy of heresies was common sense," thinks Winston Smith. With double the heresies we have half as much sense.

In *1984* the party teaches that "Sexual intercourse is to be looked on as a slightly disgusting minor operation, like having an enema." But now we've got both #MeToo *and* chastity education in the public school curriculum.

Orwell described life in the year 1984 as "decaying, dingy cities where underfed people shuffled to and fro in leaky shoes, in patched-up nineteenth-century houses that smelt always of cabbage." A fair description of antifa locales in Portland, Oregon, or hip, artisanal Brooklyn. On the other hand, it's also not too different than the rust belts and trailer parks from which the alt-right pours forth.

"We make the laws of nature," the Inner Party interrogator and torturer O'Brien tells Winston. That sounds to me like both sides of the LeftRight climate change debate.

Likewise we have doubled our Thought Police forces, with one squadron apprehending visiting lecturers who fail to address college students in Newspeak and another squad circulating among Republicans in the House of Representatives arresting any notion that they can be reelected without Trumpthink.

But what is the goal, what is the objective of the LeftRight Party? Why do they oppress and overpower us? (Or, rather, why do they trick us into oppressing and overpowering ourselves?)

Orwell goes straight to the point. O'Brien tells Winston, "Power is not a means; it is an end . . . The object of power is power."

What the LeftRight Party wants is power. And what will the LeftRight Party do to us with its power?

Again, Orwell is clear. O'Brien asks:

"How does one man assert his power over another, Winston?"

Winston thought. "By making him suffer," he said.

"Exactly. By making him suffer. Unless he is suffering, how can you know that he is obeying your will and not his own? Power is inflicting pain and humiliation."

And thus Orwell neatly summarizes our choice in the current presidential election. Will you vote for pain? Or for humiliation?

Whose Bright Idea Was It
to Make Sure That Every Idiot
in the World Was in Touch
with Every Other Idiot?

Social media comes in for a lot of other criticism as well. The big corporations that operate social media platforms have the ethics of opioid addicts with jobs as Oxycontin pharmaceutical sales reps.

User privacy is equivalent to getting a prostate exam in the middle of Times Square on New Year's Eve while you and your urologist ride the ball drop.

Social media turns us into easy victims of fraud and financial manipulation. (Darn it, of all the Nigerian government officials, I spam blocked the one who *actually* had $100 million that needed to be wired to my bank account.)

Social media is giving young people a bad case of "phone face" with a big, permanent Samsung Galaxy Note 9 pimple between their eyes. And it makes our kids into victims of bullies or perpetrators of bullying—depending on whether our kids are dorks or jerks, and in my experience every kid is both.

Social media polarizes our politics by allowing us all—no matter how wrong we are about a political issue—to find a large, enthusiastic group of people who are even wronger.

But those are the small problems with social media. There's a bigger problem. Consider just the top six Internet social networks.

Facebook—2.3 billion users

YouTube—1.9 billion users

WhatsApp—1.5 billion users

Facebook Messenger—1.3 billion users

WeChat—1 billion users

Instagram—another billion users

Plus there are at least sixteen other social networks with more than 100 million users each. Do the math. No, don't. *Stop* the math! Quit adding. With just the top six we've already reached a tally of 9 billion social media accounts. *And there are only 7.5 billion people on the planet earth.*

We've run out of things to talk about—1.5 billion social media posts ago.

The first broadly functional social media network, SixDegrees, wasn't introduced until 1997. At the height of its popularity it had 3.5 million subscribers. But since then we've created a world where we can hear what everybody's got to say.

Nobody's got *that* much to say.

Social media is CB radio. "Breaker, breaker." "You copy?" "I'm wall to wall and treetop tall." "What's your handle, good buddy?" Except it lacks the intellectual depth. "And that's a big 10-4."

We're just blithering. The brilliant media theory philosopher Marshall McLuhan said in 1964, "The medium is the message." (Or, as my mom put it long before Marshall McLuhan had been heard of, "It's not what you say it's how you say it.") If the medium is *blather by the billions*, the message is a load of crap.

Crap and vicious crap. Crap thrown with intent.

McLuhan foresaw the World Wide Web almost thrity years before the fact. He was not sanguine about its yackety-yackety-yak. In his 1962 book *The Gutenberg Galaxy*, McLuhan wrote:

> The world has become a *computer*, an electronic brain, exactly as an infantile piece of *science fiction* . . . And as our senses have gone outside us . . . we shall at once move into a phase of panic terrors, exactly befitting a small world of tribal drums, total interdependence, and superimposed co-existence . . . Terror is the normal state of any oral society, for in it everything affects everything all the time.

McLuhan predicted that advances in electronic media would create a "Global Village." At the time a lot of us thought that was a swell idea. McLuhan didn't.

In a 1977 program on Ontario TV McLuhan was interviewed by the Canadian journalist Mike McManus.

McManus: But it seems, Dr. McLuhan, that this tribal world is not friendly.

McLuhan: The closer you get together the more you like each other? There is no evidence of that in any situation we've ever heard of. When people get close together, they get more and more savage and impatient with each other.

In the middle of the past century there was a quaint idea that what the world needed was "communication." If only parents and children could *communicate*, the Generation Gap would be bridged with a hug.

If only white folks and black folks could *communicate*, the struggle for civil rights and integration would end in handshakes and backslapping.

If only we had "cultural exchange" so that the ordinary people of the United States and the Soviet Union could *communicate* . . . Therefore an exceedingly dull publication called *Soviet Life* showed up in American public libraries and a sort of bowdlerized version of *Life* magazine, *Amerika*, published by the U.S. State Department, showed up—or didn't—somewhere—or not—in the U.S.S.R. (The Cold War was not noticeably defrosted.)

All of this was nicely satirized in the 1967 movie *Cool Hand Luke* when prison warden Strother Martin beats the (decent and freedom-loving) crap out of Paul Newman and says, "What we've got here is . . . failure to communicate."

Or, as it was put more succinctly by Joan Rivers: "Can we talk?"

The hazards of talking too much are proverbial. The *Oxford Dictionary of American Proverbs* has fifty-two entries on the subject of "talk" and "talking." All of them admonishments.

> *Big talk will not boil the pot.*
> *Idle talk burns the porridge.*
> *Talk is easy, work is hard.*
> *Big talker, little doer.*
> *Who talks the most knows the least.*
> *People who wouldn't think of talking with their mouths*
>   *full often speak with their heads empty.*
> *A child learns to talk in two years, but it takes him sixty*
>   *years to learn to keep his mouth shut.*
> *Money talks, but all it ever says is goodbye.*

Or, as my mom also said, "Not everything that runs through your mind has to pour out your mouth."

With social media, we've done something worse than create a world where we can hear what everybody says. We've created a world where we can hear what everybody *thinks*.

And that's a scary thought. Scary enough that it's the premise of a terrifying 2008 YA novel by Patrick Ness called *The Knife of Never Letting Go*. Ness describes the phenomenon, which is driving his twelve-year-old protagonist mad, as an "ever present cascade of 'Noise.'"

Hearing what's going on in other people's minds is also the premise of a 2000 romcom starring Mel Gibson and Helen Hunt, *What Women Want*, which is also scary—in the sense of being a frighteningly bad movie.

Mel Gibson gets a shock from his electric hair dryer. (He has a hairstyle from the year 2000.) This causes him to be able to hear what women think. They aren't thinking good things about him. Being that it's a romantic comedy—as opposed to something closer to real life such as a terrifying young adult novel—this makes Mel Gibson (after a lot of predictable plot) a better person.

Although not in real life. In 2006 Gibson got in trouble for an anti-Semitic outburst at a Los Angles County sheriff's deputy who'd pulled Mel over for suspected DUI.

After we got to hear what Mel was thinking, he had to enter a substance abuse recovery program. Which should remind us that we've always had a way to hear what everybody thinks. It's called booze.

Sure puts my mouth in gear. Meanwhile, what social media should be drinking is a big cup of shut up.

A Brief Historical Digression on How Communication Has Devolved

If there be e-volution, there surely is de-volution, a degradation of the species.

—sermon by Rev. Hugh S. Carpenter, 1882

They tell us that
We lost our tails
Evolving up
From little snails
I say it's all
Just wind in sails

—Devo, 1977

The computer is a handy device. It's terrific for looking up who played Wally Cleaver on *Leave It to Beaver*. But the computer is essentially meaningless to wisdom, learning, and sense.

My laptop may be a great technological improvement on my old IBM Selectric. (Wally was played by Tony Dow—I just Googled it.) But there is no historical indication that technological improvements in the way we inscribe our ideas lead to improvement in the wisdom, learning, and sense of the ideas themselves.

The opposite case can be made. When words had to be carved in stone, we got the Ten Commandments. When we needed to make our own ink and chase a goose around the yard to obtain a quill, we got William Shakespeare. When the fountain pen was invented, we got Henry James. When the typewriter came along, we got Jack Kerouac. And with the advent of the smartphone keypad we got Donald Trump on Twitter.

It's not just the written word that exhibits "degradation of the species." The quality of what's communicated seems to decline steadily with every advance in the ease of communicating. And the decline started from the get-go.

Samuel Morse successfully demonstrated the telegraph in 1844. The first words he sent down the wire had gravitas, were thought-provoking, and possessed a literary (King James Bible, Numbers 23:23) pedigree:

"What hath God wrought."

But by 1876, when Alexander Graham Bell invented the telephone, messaging had already turned prosaic. The first words spoken into a phone were:

"Mr. Watson—come here—I want to see you."

And Thomas Watson was all the way over in the next room. He could probably hear Bell just fine through the doorway—in case you thought your kid texting you in the kitchen from the breakfast nook was something new.

(Poor Tom, never remembered as anything but Alexnder's butt boy, when in fact he took his phone company profits and founded one of the largest shipyards in America.)

In 1901, Guglielmo Marconi made the first long-distance radio transmission. What did he have to say?

"s"

That's it. Or, to put it literally (Marconi was using the Morse code developed by Samuel Morse and Alfred Vail):

...

And Marconi was a real chatterbox compared to the man who invented television in 1927, Philo T. Farnsworth (really, that was his name). We can't analyze the content of the first TV broadcast because it didn't have any. What showed up on Farnsworth's cathode ray tube was:

———

A straight line. Which is, I suppose, some kind of "intellectual level," so to speak. But Farnsworth soon brought the intellectual level of television further down to where it has remained ever since. The second thing he broadcast was:

$

He put a dollar sign in front of his primitive camera because—according to what I read on the Internet—an investor asked, "When are we going to see some dollars in this thing, Farnsworth?"

Which brings us to that Internet, which tells me—with no apparent embarrassment—that the first word ever to appear on itself was:

"lo"

In 1969 a UCLA student named Charley Kline tried to transmit the command "login" to a Stanford Research Institute computer on ARPANET. This caused the system to crash, and all that came through was "lo." About an hour later (if you think the people in tech support are bad now, imagine how bad they were when they didn't exist) the "gin" arrived.

And I am still waiting for the olive and the vermouth.

And While I'm Ranting Against the Digital Age Let Me Not Forget to Excoriate an Aspect of Social Media that Lacks Even Sociability . . .

On the Fresh Hell of the Internet of Things

Our belongings as well as our selves are online. The world is filling with "smart devices." A tirade on these gadgets might seem to be off the topic of America having worked itself into a state of angry perplexity. But, in abetting furious confusion, they work for me.

To requote Marshall McLuhan abbreviated: "The world has become a computer, and as our senses go outside ourselves we move into a phase of panic terrors."

I'm not exactly panicked or terrorized by the Echo Dot that I (unaccountably) received for my seventy-third birthday but I take McLuhan's point.

I'm an ordinary old married man. I'm used to everybody being smarter than me. Major media outlets are full of reporting and editorials about how stupid my

political, social, and cultural ideas are. I long ago con-
ceded the point about who has the brains in the family.
A twenty-fifth wedding anniversary proves it. I have
children ranging from sixteen to twenty-two. They know
everything. I have hunting dogs. *I* can't tell if there's a
pheasant in a corn row forty feet away.

I *suppose* I'm smarter than the chickens I keep. Although they've got a swell coop, a spacious yard fenced
high and low to protect them from life's perils, free food
every day, and they're not doing a damn thing—such as
laying eggs—in return. So I suppose not.

But now it isn't just every*body* that's smarter than
me. Every*thing* is smarter too.

Or so I'm told—by a certain smart-alecky smart device in my lap being a five-pound know-it-all. (Although
it turns into a moron if I spill a cup of coffee on its
keyboard.) Forgoing that temptation, I Google and find
PC Magazine's "Best Smart Home Devices." The article
beings,

> What if all the devices in your life could connect to
> the internet? Not just computers and smartphones,
> but *everything:* clocks, speakers, lights, doorbells,
> cameras, windows, window blinds, hot water heat-
> ers, appliances, cooking utensils, you name it. And
> what if those devices could all communicate, send
> you information, and take your commands?

Let me tell you what the "what" is in this "what if"
scenario. I'd forget my password. That's what.

Also, I do not care to start having conversations with inanimate objects. I'm at an age where this is the kind of behavior that could cause my wife and children to stage an intervention. ("He forgot his password and his password is 'password.'") I'd wind up in the Memory Care unit of the local nursing home.

Even assuming I remember my password and assuming I'm allowed to remain in my own house with in-home senior care, I'm still baffled by *PC Magazine*'s list.

Video Doorbell Enhances my household security by giving me an on-screen real-time image of who's at the door. Really? There's this thing that never needs recharging and works perfectly when the Internet crashes. It's called a window. I look through it. Also, I have a 12-gauge pump.

Smart Thermostat The temperature can be adjusted from anywhere with wifi. Oh good. Now my wife and I can argue about whether it's too hot in our living room or too cold in our living room even when we're on vacation hundreds of miles from our living room.

Smart Microwave So smart that when you touch "defrost" it tells you, "Quit nuking the Swanson Hungry-Man Classic Fried Chicken frozen TV dinners and learn how to cook something healthy, Fatso."

Smart Bathroom Scale If it's in league with the Smart Microwave and thinks telling me what I really weigh is a smart idea, it's about to find out just how heavy the big back tire on my John Deere is.

Smart Vacuum Cleaner It doesn't look so smart anymore. The iRobot Roomba i7+ may have AI but my black Lab has teeth.

Smart Lawn Mower Who needs a $2,430 Husqvarna Automower 315XH that mows the lawn automatically when you've got a teen who mows the lawn automatically (if a lot of nagging counts as automation) in return for the car keys? (Although there is the matter of that $2,430 body and fender repair from when Buster backed into the phone pole.)

Home Surveillance Camera 5g hi-def 2.0 version. I mentioned I have children. Do you think I *want* to know what goes on when they're home and my wife and I are not? Besides, they leave evidence from which even Sherlock's dimwit sidekick Dr. Watson could make accurate deductions. "I detect that someone has tried to flush a pony keg down the toilet."

And that's just some of the latest stuff from the "Internet of Things." What kind of things will get smart next? Are we ready for "Smarty Pants"? This is a pair of slacks that will send you a text message: "We really *do* make your butt look big."

The Internet of Things—when I hear the phrase I feel like things are not only getting too smart but starting to gang up on me. It makes my flesh crawl. Which is medical information that my smartwatch would send directly to my in-home senior caregiver. If I owned a smartwatch. Which I don't because I own Chicago's first album, released in 1969, when people were still skeptical about the benefits of technology, even the analog kind with very limited intelligence.

> As I was walking down the street one day
> A man came up to me and asked me what the time was
>   on my watch
> And I said
> Does anybody really know what time it is?
> Does anybody really care?
> If so I can't imagine why
> We've all got time enough to cry

Cry, "Enough already with the Internet of Things!" Plus there's this to consider . . . Two ordinary old married men are playing golf.

First Golfer: Take a look at this golf ball. Doesn't matter how bad you hook or slice. It's got a flashing red light and a beeper and a GPS chip and a Bluetooth tracking locator and a camera that sends you a selfie of its location.

Second Golfer: Wow! Where did you get that golf ball?

First Golfer: I found it.

Lessons in Fake News from
Two Old Masters of the Form

On February 17, 2017, I noted down one of Donald Trump's Twitter messages. This is not something I usually do. The words that come from this president don't tend to be informative. Not for nothing do "ignorant" and "ignore" have the same Latin root. And the meaning of the phrase in Psalm 8 "Out of the mouth of babes and sucklings" is not that the infantile have anything substantive to say. The meaning is that even squalling brats can recognize what's clearly evident. In the case of Psalm 8 this is the glory of God. In the case of our squalling brat president evidence doesn't exist. It's fake news. Or, as Trump would put it, "FAKE NEWS."

So, as I was saying, I copied this particular tweet into my "Trump Miscellany" notebook:

"The FAKE NEWS media (failing nytimes, NBCNews, CBS, CNN) is not my enemy, it is the enemy of the American People!"

This was nothing Trump hadn't said before while he was campaigning. And it wasn't anything he wouldn't say again—and again—during his presidency. But that particular tweet, just a month after he was inaugurated, seemed gnomic, apothegmatic, and—not to tease the man for his near illiteracy—pithy.

What was also interesting was that Trump might have gotten it right about the oppositional relationship between the news and the citizenry.

One of the great newsmen of all time, H. L. Mencken, agreed. In *Heathen Days*, the third volume of his autobiography, published in 1943, Mencken says, "The plain people . . . are always, in fact, against newspapers." And to make a further, prescient case for the yet unborn Trump, Mencken went on to say, "and they are always in favor of what reformers call political corruption. They believe that it keeps money in circulation, and makes for a spacious and stimulating communal life."

Certainly the past four years have been stimulating, and news coverage of Trump and his administration has been spacious, to say the least, and plenty of money has been kept in circulation.

As for "FAKE NEWS," it has been with us for quite a while. Mencken has a gleeful passage in his autobiography's second volume, *Newspaper Days*, published in 1941, about reporting for the *Baltimore Herald* during a slow news week in 1903:

> A wild man was reported loose in the woods over
> Baltimore's northern city line, with every dog barking
> for miles around, and all women and children locked

up. I got special delight out of the wild man, for I had invented him myself.

Another lesson from Mencken is that we should be wary about "feuds" between politicians and the media. In *Heathen Days* Mencken recounts how, during the 1910s, the newspaper where he was a reporter and where he would remain for the rest of his working reporter days, the *Baltimore Sun*, was engaged in a huge political quarrel with Baltimore's mayor J. Harry Preston. Never mind that both Preston and the *Sun's* editor were die-hard Democrats.

According to Mencken, if Preston "proposed to enlarge the town dog-pound" the *Sun* would denounce it "as an assault upon the solvency of Baltimore, the comity of nations, and the Ten Commandments." And if the *Sun* editorialized in favor of clean alleys "Preston went about the ward clubs warning his heelers that the proposal was only the opening wedge for anarchy, atheism, and cannibalism."

Mencken confesses, "My own share in this campaign of defamation was large and assiduous." And then he says, "I was fond of [Preston], thought he was doing well as mayor, and often met him amicably at beer-parties."

Mark Twain was also an old newsman. He instructs us to be equally wary of feuds between media outlets themselves. In an 1869 piece for the *Buffalo Express*, "Journalism in Tennessee," Twain wrote, with perhaps slight exaggeration, about witnessing a confrontation between the editor in chief of the *Morning Glory and Johnson County War-Whoop* and a Colonel Bascom, proprietor of a rival paper, the *Thunderbolt and Battle-Cry of Freedom*.

> "Both pistols rang out their fierce clamor at the same instant. The chief lost a lock of hair, and the Colonel's bullet ended its career in the fleshy part of my thigh. The Colonel's left shoulder was clipped a little. They fired again. Both missed their men this time, but I got my share, a shot in the arm. At the third fire both gentlemen were wounded slightly, and I had a knuckle chipped . . . They then talked about the elections and the crops a while, and I fell to tying up my wounds.

Maybe we should go ask Tucker Carlson and Lawrence O'Donnell how the crops—and the elections—are doing. You first.

Woke to the Sound
of Laughter

Puritanism is back—and you're welcome to it. I applaud the New Piety and want to tell twenty-first-century thought leaders that your current fashion for sanctimoniousness, earnest solemnity, and taking everything very seriously indeed is just what's needed.

Humor depends upon irking the dour, the censorious, and the po-faced. Now there's a fresh abundance of calamity howlers, bluenoses, and vinegar pusses to provoke.

This is a great relief. For most of the previous century lemon-sucking prudes were scarce and sadly out of style. Life was mirth-deprived.

World War I was followed by a licentious riot of amoral libertinism with the collapse of ethical norms, societal conventions, plain good manners, and religious convictions.

Nothing was sacrosanct. This turned laughter into hard work, like going to see *Waiting for Godot* and waiting for the punch lines. Or skating over the thin ice on a river of despair in the novels of Evelyn Waugh. Or fearfully suspecting, with *Dr. Strangelove*, *Catch-22*, and *Slaughterhouse-Five*, that levity might be a symptom of mental illness.

Lacking icons, the iconoclastic joker is just a crazed person trying to break things in a safe space—his padded cell. Without taboos Tabu is a perfume, available in better stores since 1932. Shortly after Tabu was introduced Cole Porter sang

In olden days, a glimpse of stocking
Was looked on as something shocking.
But now, God knows,
Anything goes.

And everything went. The years from 1918 to 2016 weren't funny. First came manic-depressive economies, then the rise of totalitarian ideologies, another world war, Mutually Assured Destruction, the antinomian violence of the 1960s, dissolution of the nuclear family, evisceration of the middle class, and people over forty wearing bicycle shorts.

Goodbye to all that (except, alas, the bicycle shorts). You stiff-necked pettifoggers have reemerged from the loosey-goosey fog bank of pre-postmodernism. Thank you. The long drought in prudery is over. Japes at Tartuffian cant can begin anew.

Jesters witnessed, with happy surprise, the rebirth of priggish shock and prissy moral indignation when a licentious riot of amoral libertinism was elected president of the United States in 2016.

(Actually, Bill Clinton was elected president in 1992. But the New Piety had yet to be proclaimed. Imagine how much more fun the Monica Lewinsky imbroglio would have been with #MeToo. Unfortunately for the sanctimoniously pious and earnestly solemn, the Clintons arrived too soon—Gadarene swine with nobody to chase them into the sea.)

But nowadays you, the woke, have perfected your pietism. You know just which conscious thoughts to decry and just what unconscious thoughts to condemn, and you even know the precise words that mustn't be used to describe any of those thoughts. For example, you disapprove of the noun "mankind." You grapple with English as if the language were a professional wrestling villain attempting to pin "womynkind" to the mat.

(Rematch to be announced. "Womyn" is considered transexclusionary by gender activists.)

To be woke is to maintain a state of mind where you are constantly and acutely alert to social injustice and permanently on the lookout for more social injustice to be alert to. Or what I would call a good reason to take a nap.

Which one would think would be perfectly acceptable since being woke doesn't seem to entail actually doing anything. But thankfully for the merry-andrew, if you're woke you must stay "conscious" in order to continually "communicate" how "vigilant" you are about "toxic masculinity," how "mindful" you're becoming about "cultural appropriation," and how "committed" you are to "no platform" people who disagree with you by, for instance, putting your vocabulary in quotation marks.

Thus each of you becomes a "social justice warrior" armed, like Samson, with the jaw of an ass.

Being woke is a parody of being born again—instead of you accepting Jesus, people like Jesus (Cisgender normative, famously well-connected father) have to accept you.

And, as to religion, it's about time we had a new one. Religion has been the mainstay of lampoon at least since Voltaire. But the old established creeds are no fit targets for jocularity—doddering congregations, frayed theologies, and sorry impoverishment from being sued for less than comical behavior. A fresh theology to poke fun at is required.

I don't understand your creed, but I enjoy it. Diversity is a wonderful new shibboleth—you must both pronounce it correctly and not pronounce it at all. Differences between religions, races, ethnicities, cultures, and various genders (after a million years with just two, dozens more have been discovered) can never be acknowledged. Then they must be celebrated.

And tolerance is a wonderful new sin. It's a modern moral lapse to practice toleration when glorification is what contemporary mores demand. Witness the shamed Colorado confectioner who, on the occasion of a gay wedding, failed the "If I knew you were coming I would have baked a cake" test.

Of course the New Piety requires up-to-date saints. Gladly there's no shortage. Martyrdom has become inclusive. Hurt feelings count. So does Joe Biden smelling your hair. Saintly relics are close at hand. You have a mental reliquary filled with splinters from the true cross of your personal victimhood.

And worship has never been easier. All you have to do by way of praise and adoration is think well of yourself. It's another new sin not to. Self-esteem is a human right. You are a good person. You are an excellent person. Look at your tattoos—you're a signed masterpiece.

But what happens if one of you wants to be more than merely holier-than-thou? All they has to do—using the plural pronoun as singular to show how grammar needs a theological correction—is recycle something. Preferably something indicating "awareness" and "engagement" such as an empty container of organic, gluten-free, non-GMO, locally sourced, fair-traded drain cleaner. Being holier-than-globally-everybody is a sustainable alternative for the progressively minded faithful.

And Charles Dudley Warner's quip "Everybody complains about the weather, but nobody does anything about it"? That is so early-Trump-campaign. Everybody *you* know is devoutly stopping climate change. The way you did when you made obeisance over the bins marked "glass," "paper," "polypropylene plastic," "polystyrene plastic," and "biodegradables"—worshiping the garbage can.

Meanwhile everybody *I* know is having a much more amusing life.

Why Kids Я Commies

*And Never Mind How the Free Market
Bankrupted that Backwards R
Big Box Store that Once Held a
Greedy Monopoly on Selling Toys*

Americaʼs young people have veered to the left. Opinion pollsters tell us so. According to a November 2019 Gallup Poll, "Since 2010 young adultsʼ positive ratings of socialism have hovered near 50%." A March 2019 Axios poll concurs, saying that 49 percent of millennials would "Prefer living in a socialist country." And *The Hill* puts it more strongly, citing an October 2019 YouGov Internet survey in a story headed, "7 in 10 Millennials Say Theyʼd Vote for a Socialist."

Traditional liberalism still exists. In a March 2018 Pew Research Center study of Americans age 22–37, 57 percent called themselves "mostly" or "consistently" liberal.

But "mostly" or "consistently" liberal may not be enough for young voters. This was evident in the 2018 congressional elections. Ten-term incumbent congressmen Michael Capuano (D. Mass.) and Joe Crowley (D. NY) were as mostly consistently liberal as they come. And they were kicked to the curb in Democratic primaries by leftists Ayanna Pressley and Alexandria Ocasio-Cortez.

What's the matter with kids today? Nothing new. A large portion of the brats, the squirts, the fuzz-faced, the moon claves, the sap-green, and the wet behind the ears have always been "Punks for Progressives."

As soon as children discover that the world isn't nice, they want to make it nicer. And wouldn't a world where everybody shares everything be nice? Aw . . . Kids are so tender-hearted.

But kids are broke—so they want to make the world nicer with *your* money. And kids don't have much control over things—so they want to make the world nicer through *your* effort. And kids are very busy being young—so it's *your* time that has to be spent making the world nicer.

For them. The greedy little bastards. Kids were thinking these exact same sweet-young-thing thoughts back in the 1960s, during my salad days (tossed green sensimilla buds). Young people probably have been thinking these same thoughts since the concept of being a "young person" was invented.

That would have been in the nineteenth century—during America's first "Progressive Era"—when mechanization liberated kids from onerous farm chores and child labor laws let them escape from child labor.

This gave young people the leisure to sit around noticing that the world isn't nice and daydreaming about how it could be made nicer with the time, effort, and money of grow-ups.

I'm all for sending them back to the factories or, at least, the barn. If I hear any socialist noise from my kids I'm going to make them get up at 4 a.m. to milk the cows. And this will be an extra-onerous farm chore because we don't have any cows, and they'll have to search for miles all over the countryside to find some.

They've got it coming. Young people are not only penniless and powerless, they're also ignorant as hell. They think of wealth as something that's limited, like the number of Hostess Ding Dongs on the 7-Eleven shelf. They think rich people got to the 7-Eleven first and gobbled all the Ding Dongs, leaving poor people to lick the plastic wrappers.

Young people don't know that more Ding Dongs can be produced. They don't know how or why more Ding Dong production is possible. And they certainly don't know how to get the cream filling inside.

(Leaving aside the wild indignation of young people about the very existence of synthetic industrial and undoubtedly poisonous food such as Ding Dongs. They eat them anyway. Watch them shop at the 7-Eleven when they think nobody's looking. But I digress.)

Young people believe that the way to obtain more wealth is to take it away from rich people. You can't do it. Well, you *can* do it. But you can only do it once.

You can take the Ding Dongs from the Hostess factory for free, but once you've eaten them you can't go back to the Hostess factory and take more Ding Dongs for free. The Hostess factory is out of business. (Which may protect our health, reduce environmental pollution, and preserve various species of animals such as the high fructose corn weevil, which, for all I know, is endangered. Although, considering that Pew Research claims even more millennials [69 percent] favor cannabis legalization than favor socialism, *somebody's* going to be sorry when they get the munchies. But I digress again.)

Young people are so ignorant about wealth that they think wealth is limited to what arrives at the 7-Eleven with the Hostess deliveryman. The reason they think this is because young people are still in school or have been recently.

School, while not without its benefits, carries the risk of over-exposure to intellectuals. And intellectuals, when it comes to understanding economic realities, are Ding Dongs.

The nineteenth century spawning of idle, dreamy, feckless young people arrived just in time for the Marxist intellectual fad. And Marxist thinking among intellectuals is a fashion trend that has never gone away.

Intellectuals like Marxism because Marx makes economics simple—the rich get their money from the poor. (How the rich manage this, since the poor by definition don't have any money, is beyond me. But never mind.)

Real economics are more complicated than anything that intellectuals can make sense of.* Also, living in an ivory tower teaches few economic lessons—even fewer now that intellectuals have banned the ivory trade.

Marxism puts inarticulate notions of a sharing-caring nicer world into vivid propaganda slogans. Slogans such as: *"From each according to his ability, to each according to his need."*** Which may be the most ridiculous political-economic idea that anybody has ever had.

My need is for Beluga caviar, a case of Chateau Haut-Brion 1961, a duplex on 5th Avenue overlooking Central Park, a bespoke suit from Gieves & Hawkes in Savile Row, a matched pair of Purdey 12-bore sidelock shot-guns, and a 1962 Ferrari 250 GTO that recently sold at Sotheby's Monterey auction for $48.4 million.

My ability is . . . Um . . . I have an excellent memory for limericks . . .

There once was a man from Nantucket . . .

What kind of totalitarian mind-meld would be required to determine everyone's abilities and needs? What kind of dictatorship body slam would be necessary to

---

* This is similar to the baseball/football conundrum. My late and much missed (and highly intellectual) friend Charles Krauthammer pointed it out. He said, "Do you know why intellectuals love baseball so much? *Because football is too hard to understand.*

** A common socialist catch phrase of the 1840s swiped by Karl Marx who felt—like Ayanna Pressley and Alexandria Ocasio-Cortez felt about Michael Capuano and Joe Crowley—that the socialists weren't socialistic enough.

distribute the goods of the able to the wants of the needy? We know what kind. The kind that the U.S.S.R and Mao's China did their best to create.

The Soviet Union and Maoist China are two more reasons that millennials love socialism. This is not because young people learned left-wing lessons from the Soviets and the Red Guards. It's because they *didn't*.

Kids don't get it that communists are bad people. It was too long ago. The Berlin Wall fell in 1989. Deng Xiaoping began market reforms in China in 1978. I have two millennial daughters. The end of the Cold War and the beginning of China's economic boom are, respectively, as distant in time from them as the Great Depression and the Coolidge administration are from me.

To millennials, hearing the U.S.S.R. and Mao's China used as examples of how socialism can go very, very wrong is like me hearing about the Kellogg-Briand Pact and the Smoot-Hawley Tariff. I *did* hear about the Kellogg-Briand Pact and the Smoot-Hawley Tariff in American History class. And I was not listening as hard as I could. Taking a guess, I'd say one was an international breakfast cereal treaty and the other had to do with the price of smoots.

For young people today, the only communist societies they know anything about* are that goofy outlier

---

* Okay, there's Venezuela. But, doing DIY opinion polling, I queried my three kids. My eldest replied by text: "OMG dad im studying 4 my art hist final ive got to memoize 35 german expressionists!!!" My middle child emailed, "Isn't it something else Trump did bad." And my youngest (who's taking Spanish) said, "Zuelas for sale?"

North Korea and Cuba, where the Marxist-Leninism comes with cheap rum, '57 Chevys, and "Guantanamera" sing-alongs.

Or, I should say, these are the only communist societies young people know anything about, *except one* . . . The communist society in which all young people grow up.

"From each according to his ability, to each according to his need" is deeply stupid and completely impractical. And yet there's a place where it works. This place is my house. And your house. And anywhere else there's a family.

To each according to his need . . . What *don't* kids need? My sixteen-year-old son needs Mom to drive to school with his lunch, his homework, and one sock. Never mind that she packed his lunch, did his homework, and washed his socks—one of which he left behind this morning along with his homework and his lunch so that she has to drive back to school even though she just returned from driving him to school.

From each according to Mom's and Dad's ability, not to mention the ability of Mom's and Dad's Visa card credit line and the bank loans we took out to pay for school tuition.

The grim truth is, kids are *born* communists.

Knowing Write
from Left

Another reason kids are communists is that they're taught to read.

Literature hates capitalism. This has nothing to do with literary elite types being fashionably lefty. Taking a guess from personal experience (albeit peripheral to anything that could be called literature), it has something to do with writers being morons about money.

Or not. Shakespeare seems to have been nobody's fool in the matter of pounds, shillings, and pence. And Shakespeare was hating capitalism while capitalism was still being invented—before "capitalist" was even a word.

The Merchant of Venice centers on a nasty portrayal of Shylock, the only worthwhile person in the play.

All the other main characters are rich layabouts, except for the titular merchant, Antonio, and he's an idiot. He's going to loan his profligate friend Bassanio 3,000 ducats (something like half a million dollars) so that Bassanio can afford to date Portia.

Meanwhile Antonio's business affairs are a mess. He's cash poor because all his capital is tied up in high-risk ventures. He's counting on huge returns from emerging market trading ventures.

Shylock, a keen-eyed financial analyst, sums up Antonio's investment portfolio: "He hath an argosy bound to Tripolis, another to the Indies . . . a third at Mexico, a fourth for England."

Libya, Southeast Asia, Mexico, and . . . England? What, exactly, is this merchant of Venice *merchandizing*? Looks to me like he's trading in boat people, smuggled rhino horns, drugs, and . . . kippered herring?

Anyway, it's left to the sensible, hardworking, put-upon Shylock to do the banking for these jerks, and if he gets carried away with his loan default penalty clause who can blame him?

Maybe literature hates capitalism because sensible, hardworking, put-upon people—unless they go nuclear like Shylock—are boring to write about.

Anyway, wide is the gate and broad is the way from Shakespeare's Shylock to Ebenezer Scrooge of Charles Dickens's *A Christmas Carol*.

The charge against Scrooge is merely that he's a lonely old man who works too hard, pays the going wage, and is skeptical about the merits of private philanthropy. We hear nothing about the glories performed by his accumulated capital—financing highways, canals, railroads, workshops, factories, business establishments, dwelling houses, and, perhaps, start-ups doing biotech research into what ails Tiny Tim.

In return for Scrooge's beneficence to society Dickens inflicts dreadful nightmares on him. (Although I'm not sure the apparition of Marley is as scary to Scrooge as Dickens wants it to be. Marley's ghost is, after all, chained to Marley's money boxes—so maybe you *can* take it with you.)

Then, at the end of the story, Dickens still isn't done torturing his innocent victim. He has Scrooge suffer a mental breakdown, a terrifying manic episode where Scrooge "walked about the streets, and watched the people hurrying to and fro, and patted children on the head, and questioned beggars, and looked down into the kitchens of houses, and up to the windows, and found that everything could yield him pleasure."

Poor Bob Cratchit doubtless had to have Ebenezer confined to Bedlam.

And off to the loony bin of anticapitalism with you, too, F. Scott Fitzgerald. In *The Great Gatsby*, a successful businessman is shown to be a howitzer among cap pistols, especially compared to the dribbling squirt gun of a narrator, Nick Carraway. Tom and Daisy Buchanan are trust fund twits. Everyone else is a nonentity.

It's Jay Gatsby who throws the fabulous parties, has the great love affair, and spends piles of money so everybody else can have fun.

That money came from somewhere. Probably from Gatsby's intelligence and diligent effort. As to the money coming from bootlegging, we have only the worthless Tom Buchanan's word to go on about that. And bootlegging requires intelligence and diligent effort (and capital) too. Also, Fitzgerald would have been writing about the "Boring Twenties" if it hadn't been for bathtub gin.

There are, of course, exceptions to the rule of litera-ture hating capitalism. There are novels, plays, and even poems about the blessings of economic liberty and the fact that private property is the basis of human freedom. But these works are rarely taught in school.

Maybe this is because the teachers are afraid to be politically incorrect. More likely it's because most pro-capitalist literature stinks.

My college-age daughter managed to find some. I got a text from her: "i LOVE this paperback im reading cause i got bored with my eng lit homework and it was laying around the dorm lounge and its called the foun-tainhead by somebody named ayn sp? rand and have u ever heard of her?"

I can't stand Ayn Rand and her fulsome overargument of the blatantly obvious. But I'm not twenty. Actually, it's an appropriate book for a youngster immersed in the groupthink liberal-quibble, squishy, faux-communal world of academia.

The Fountainhead is wildly romantic. Genius architect Howard Roark—a sort of Frank Lloyd Wright with a libertarian hair up his ass—would rather pull the world down around his head than submit to the diktat of col-lectivist architectural mediocrity.

In fact, given the fiery romance between Roark and Dominique Francon (Ayn in thin—and better-looking—disguise), *The Fountainhead* is even a bit of a bodice ripper. But what really gets torn to pieces is the shabby economic underwear beneath the fine fabric of good literature.

So my daughter will also like Rand's *Atlas Shrugged*. This is another lousy book. But it has what's among the best plot premises ever as capitalism's creative geniuses all go on strike.

Twenty-five years ago my wife and I took the Trans-Siberian Railway across the former Soviet Union. The country hadn't recovered from communism. (And much of it hasn't yet.) The cities, towns, and farms were a gloomy, depressing mess.

My wife grew up in the conventionally conservative capitalist milieu of suburban Connecticut. But until our trip to Russia she hadn't been particularly interested in political economics. She took *Atlas Shrugged* along to read on the trip (mostly on the theory of "long ride, long book"). And she kept glancing up from the pages and looking out the train window and saying, "So *that's* what happened to this country!"

Or if you prefer your pro-capitalist reading to be set in the dank past rather than the ghastly present or grim future there's *A Connecticut Yankee in King Arthur's Court* by Mark Twain.

This is arguably Twain's worst work. It's haphazardly plotted, sloppily written, and the comedy is force-fed. But, again, the premise is brilliant.

The manager of a New England factory, with all his mechanical and entrepreneurial skills, time travels to the Middle Ages where ignorance, superstition, and a violent aristocracy rule. Also everything turns out to be filthy dirty back then. The Connecticut Yankee shows the Knights of the Round Table how to keep their table from wobbling and another thing or two.

Twain reminds his readers (if a little too often) how much the world owes to free enterprise, ingenuity, reason, scientific inquiry, and all the other wonderful things that have happened since people escaped serfdom and slavery and became self-actuated and self-interested (hence capitalist) individuals.

There is, I'm glad to say, at least one work of pro-capitalist literature that is literature, even though today it would be categorized as YA fiction, and any child who actually likes to read keeps as far away from that section of the library as possible lest a terrifying copy of Patrick Ness's *The Knife of Never Letting Go* be thrust upon him or her. Furthermore, its author stands so notoriously accused of being imperialist, colonialist, and racist that an attempt at a library checkout of *Captains Courageous* by Rudyard Kipling would probably land the kid in counseling.

I bought my son a copy of his own (never mind that that probably put me on some sort of Amazon. com blacklist).

The story begins with a spoiled young brat, scion of a railroad magnate (and about the age of my son), out on the fantail of a luxury liner puffing on an illicit cigar. He gets dizzy and sick, falls overboard, and is rescued by a fishing boat.

The fishermen could care less who the brat's father is. They've got fishing to do. And they won't be back to port for months. If the brat wants a bunk and three meals a day he'd better learn how to fish.

Capitalism is a coin with two sides. The brat knew about "heads"—capital. Now he learns about "tails"—labor.

In the end, the wealthy dad rewards the fishing boat crew for saving his son. And the son is rewarded with an education in the kind of hard work that made his dad wealthy.

I'm not saying my son is a spoiled brat. But after he reads *Captains Courageous*, if he *acts* like a spoiled brat, I can tell him, "Go Fish."

Or I can recite a nursery rhyme to him. I said there was pro-capitalist poetry, and I can prove it by quoting Ogden Nash (1902–71), perhaps the greatest author of light verse in the English language. Nash wrote the poem "One From One Leaves Two" in response to the New Deal.

Abracadabra, thus we learn
The more you create, the less you earn.
The less you earn, the more you're given,
The less you lead, the more you're driven,

. . .

The more you earn, the less you keep,
And now I lay me down to sleep.
I pray the Lord my soul to take
If the tax-collector hasn't got it before I wake.

Educating My Kids

I want my kids to believe in getting a good education. This, as distinct from *getting an education*. You can
get that anywhere. In the gutter where I did. At home.
Maybe even in the classroom.

A good education is another matter. And possessing
faith in the value of a good education is another matter
yet. I want my children to have facts, facility for critical
thinking, and analytical capabilities. And I also want
them to be convinced that putting these things to work
is a worthwhile activity.

That is a lot to ask in a world where, seemingly,
facts are fads, criticism is cancel culture, and analysis
has returned to its Greek root, *lysis*, "a loosing," mostly
of the verbal bowels.

I have a friend who sends his kids to Catholic school,
partly because he's Catholic, but mostly because he lives
in a big American city where—as in all big American
cities—the public schools suck.

I asked my friend, "Are the Catholic schools any
good?"

"No," he said. "But the kids aren't taught anything that I have to unteach them when they come home."

And that's pretty much all I've asked from the schools where I've sent my three children. I've been lucky. They haven't come home needing to dis-learn much.

There was one occasion, at the kids' sort-of-but-not-too-Montessori-ish grade school, when a teacher answered a second-grader's question about the difference between Democrats and Republicans by saying, "Democrats care about people."

Fortunately for my police blotter record, another parent blew her top before I had a chance to blow mine. Called to the principal's office, the teacher's ears were pinned back and her hair was scorched off by an angry mom yelling, "Democrats care about 'The People'! Democrats hate *people*! Republicans care about people and hate 'The People'! Especially you!"

And last year the prep school where my daughter went had "Unconscious Bias Day"—all classes were excused in favor of required attendance at six hours of lectures, assemblies, and discussion groups devoted to the above-named topic.

This is a traditional New England prep school. Which is to say it is resolutely multicultural in curriculum, painstakingly inclusivity-insistent, and so diversity-sensitive that it grapples with whether the use of chopsticks is cultural appropriation when international students from China use them. Meanwhile, of course, the school preserves the age-old customs and mores of rich WASPs. A young man can appear in the classroom dressed like Princess Di and no one will say a word, but he will be sent back to his dorm if he wears jeans and a collarless shirt.

I said to my daughter, "Is there bias at your school?"

She said, "Oh, gosh no. Nobody's prejudiced or bigoted or anything like that."

"In that case," I said, "why not just have 'Unconscious Day'?"

Schools haven't taught my kids many bad things. On the other hand, there are many good things schools haven't taught my kids either.

Today's students can list every injustice in America but can't name a justice of the Supreme Court. I exaggerate. There's Ruth Bader Ginsburg, but I'm willing to bet that none of RBG's student fans can explain what she does for a living.

They think John Calvin had a talking toy tiger named Hobbes. Of Thomas Hobbes they've never heard at all. They know about Martin Luther King but have no idea who Martin Luther was. They believe Alexander Hamilton's *Federalist Papers* rhymed.

Today's students are fully conversant with Title IX of the Higher Education Act of 1968 but are fuzzy on the details of Articles I through VII of the U.S. Constitution, not to mention Amendments I through X—in particular II.

Furthermore, Title IX aside, they don't know their Roman numerals, and they can't write—or read—longhand.

They are cognizant of the origins of poverty but ignorant of the origins of wealth. Their instruction has been in "dark Satanic Mills" not John Stuart Mill. They wouldn't know Adam Smith from Adam.

And even knowing Adam from Eve is a pedagogical conundrum these days. Or so I gather. I haven't heard any direct reports. While I enjoy embarrassing my kids as much as the next dad, I've never gone so far as to ask them, "What did you learn in sex ed class today?"

The students have absorbed endless lessons about the horrors of war but would be baffled if they encountered the quotation "make a desolation and call it peace." Not that they're likely to be assigned to read Tacitus.

Instead they are assigned to read about the detrimental effects of Eurocentric patriarchal imperialism. What they read is true enough, no doubt. But no instructor would dare to assign "The White Man's Burden," in which the previously mentioned Rudyard Kipling writes about the detrimental effects of Eurocentric patriarchal imperialism. (Albeit Rudyard was concerned with the detrimental effects *on* Eurocentric patriarchal imperialists.)

And, come to think of it, I don't believe any of my children have ever been assigned to read a poem that rhymed. (Although they have seen *Hamilton*.)

Furthermore . . . as long as I'm fuming let's not close my chimney flue . . . today's students know all about climate change but spend too much time indoors staring at screens to know anything about weather.

Thus today's students are graduating from school too stupid to come in out of the rain. But so did we. So did everyone. That's the way it's always been. We don't get much of our education in school.

This leaves me in charge of the education my kids get *outside* school . . . I'm lying. My wife is in charge of that. And my kids can be damn thankful for it. But I try to do my little bit.

I give them two rules: mind your own business and keep your hands to yourself. I call these "The Bill and Hillary Clinton Rules." Mind your own business, Hillary. And, Bill, keep your hands to yourself.

Then I invoke the Fairness Precept. This began with my eldest daughter, a child much given to exclamations of "That's not fair!" One day, when she was about eight or nine and had worked herself into a huge snit about the unfairness of something or other, I lost my patience and snapped at her.

"Not fair?" I said. "You're cute. That's not fair. Your parents are pretty well off. That's not fair. You were *born in America*. THAT'S not fair. Honey, you'd better get down on your knees and pray to God that things don't start getting *fair* for you!"

Finally I teach them about hypocrisy. I teach by example. My mentor on the subject was my old friend (and colleague at the late, lamented *Weekly Standard* where our conservatism was merely of the half-baked kind rather than being on fire and burning everything to a cinder as is the fashion with conservatism these days) Andy Ferguson.

Andy's children are older than mine. When his were in junior high and mine were still little, I asked Andy what he was going to say when he was asked—as he inevitably would be—"Dad, did you take drugs?"

Andy, a fellow survivor of the Better Living Through Chemistry era, replied, "I'll say I never took any drugs, ever."

"Andy," I said, "what about that photo of you on the mantle from the 1970s, with your hair down to your butt and a guitar?"

"I'll say I was playing in a band that performed a folk mass at church."

"But Andy," I said, "you've published books where you've *written* about being stoned out of your gourd."

"Reading is part of a good education," Andy said, "but when it comes to reading there's one thing you can count on with your kids. They will *never* read anything written by their fathers."

Which presumably includes what I'm writing here. Therefore I have told my children that I never took drugs, never had sex until I was married to their mom, and that when I was a kid I made my bed every morning before I left for school.

If the kids believe that, they'll believe anything. They might even believe in getting a good education.

My Own Lousy Education

And How It May Be of Aid to the Nation

The dictionary definition of education is "The process of training and developing the knowledge, mind, character, etc., especially by formal schooling." I am unprocessed.

I can't exactly say I'm not educated. I have a college degree. But it's in the liberal arts. What knowledge I possess is not trained and developed. Neither is my mind, my character, or—as best I can tell—my etc.

In other words, I don't know how to do anything. I can't build a building. I can't design a rocket. I can't do math: I can't do arithmetic beyond the first part of the multiplication tables and I don't know how much a whole mess of 9's are. I can't cure your ills or drill your teeth or represent you in a court of law when you sue me for medical malpractice. I can't invest or speculate. (That is, I can't do so successfully.) I can't turn $1 into $1.01 even with the one-year Treasury rate at 1.54 percent. I can't fix a flat on your car. (Wait, I *can* fix it, if you'll let me roll your car forward a foot or two. Your tire is flat on only one side. I learned that when I took "Physics for Poets.")

I never studied a subject that has been applicable to my adult life except Abnormal Psych, and let's not go into details about that.

I was an English major because I was paging through the course catalogue and I saw "English" and I thought, "Hey, I *speak* that!"

I chose my courses in college according to what time of day the class met, adhering to the rule, "You can't drink in learning before you drink lunch."

And I graduated *cum laude* and Phi Beta Kappa. I am ignorant—but I'm good at it.

And that's the enormous advantage of a liberal arts education. You can't spend four (or five or six) years of college picking only courses that you can bluff your way through without learning to . . .

It may say "B.A." on my diploma but what I've got a degree in is "B.S." I can talk the shingles off a barn roof.

Or, as the case actually turned out, I can talk them back on. That is, yes, I'd be smarter if I had a STEM (science, technology, engineering, and mathematics) education. If I had studied trigonometry I would have realized that cutting down a fifty-foot pine tree that was twenty feet from my barn might result in certain sine, cosine, tangent, and crushed barn roof results. No, I don't know a hypotenuse from a possum belly.

But . . . you should have heard me with the insurance adjuster. Euclid, Archimedes, and Pythagoras put together weren't a patch on me. (Even less so since they'd be talking to the insurance adjuster in ancient Greek.)

By the time I got done the insurance company had not only paid for a new barn roof, it paid for a new barn to go under it *and* a new chain saw *and* a new pine tree *and* six cows to replace the cows that would have been killed when the barn roof collapsed if I'd had any cows.

I'm ignorant—but I'm good at it.

And the world should be thankful for all the liberal arts graduates who are just as good as I am at B.S. Think of all the things that we owe to B.S. Think of all the things that would be impossible without B.S.

Art

Literature

Rap music

Dating

Marriage

Having a talk with your son about the birds and bees

Advertising

Marketing

Sales

Tech company IPOs

And don't start making this list because it expands at a speed faster than *Star Trek*'s USS *Enterprise* at warp 9, which is 729 times the speed of light, which is B.S. I pulled off a website on the Internet, which wouldn't have any websites if it weren't for B.S.

*   *   *

Let us examine just two examples. First, politics.
I'll draw a box.

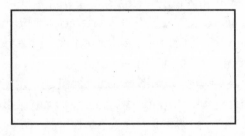

Look into the box. That's politics without B.S.

How would we be governed? Who could be elected? Imagine a candidate giving a B.S.-free stump speech: "No, I *can't* fix public education. The problem isn't funding or teachers' unions or vouchers or lack of computer equipment in the classroom. The problem is your damn kids."

Our executive, legislative, and judicial branches would cease to function. Our political institutions would be "Bare ruin'd choirs, where late the sweet birds [full of B.S.] sang."

The America that the world knows would disappear. ISIS would pop back to life and hold sway from Baghdad to Berlin. What the Islamic State didn't pillage the Islamic Republic of Iran would plunder. Vladimir Putin would leave off mere meddling and install himself, midst bathroom fixtures of gold, in New York's hastily renamed Putin Tower. Xi Jinping would be general secretary of the Communist Party of China, chief executive of Hong Kong, president of Taiwan, and mayor of Cupertino, California.

But perhaps politics isn't the best example. There's too much of it that would be good riddance. Let's take the example of all the hard subjects I so assiduously avoided in college, the dreaded STEMs—where one was tested with real questions and was expected to give real answers.

I'd argue that science, technology, engineering, and mathematics are also dependant on B.S.

Not that there's any B.S. *in* these fields. (Well, there is—but there shouldn't be.) Rather, the problem is who funds science, technology, engineering, and mathematics?

Usually, it's fools. Like me. We who are full of B.S. are the people who rise to be corporate chief executives, presidents of universities, and high plenipotentiaries holding the public purse strings.

Poor Jim Bridenstine, the NASA administrator, has to go before a congressional budget committee and say, "We need $10 billion for the James Webb Space Telescope so that we can peer deep into the universe and investigate across the fields of astronomy and cosmology to observe some of the most distant events and objects in the universe, such as the formation of the first galaxies."

Congressman: "Why? Are there voters out there?"

Jim: "Um . . ."

And this is where Jim needs B.S. He needs somebody like me to rush to his side.

Jim: "Perhaps I should let my staff member Junior Space Cadet O'Rourke explain the further benefits of the James Webb Space Telescope."

Congressman: "Let the witness be sworn in."

Me: "The Honorable Representative will be pleased to know that, besides its telescopic properties, the James Webb Space Telescope also employs an eight-foot array of mirrors which, if the situation requires, can be reversed to collect solar rays and focus them in an intense beam directed at Fox News causing the network to pop like a kernel of Orville Redenbacher's in a twelve hundred watt microwave."

Congressman: "Ten billion dollars? Okay."

What We Can Learn
from the Sixties Drug Culture

Maybe the answer to America's current state of angry perplexity is "Everybody must get stoned." It's certainly an idea that's trending. But I was around the last time we tried that. And perhaps this is an historical period that we should reexamine.

"If you can remember the sixties you weren't there" is a quote variously attributed to Grace Slick, Dennis Hopper, Robin Williams, and a bunch of other people because . . . nobody from back then can remember anything.

I'm a veteran of the 1960s "drug culture." At least I suppose so. I *was* there, a nineteen-year-old college kid during the Summer of Love. And I wasn't some student senate, frat boy, ROTC, squaresville college kid. I was fully onboard the Magical Mystery Tour. It's just that I don't recall much about it. Where were we going in the "bong bus"? What did we do when we got there? Who else was along for the ride? And why, when I try to think of their names, do they all seem to have been called "Groovy" and "Sunshine"? Oh my gosh, I hope I wasn't driving.

Fifty-three years later everything is a purple haze—
so to speak. Today there's another "drug culture" in
progress. And in an attempt to learn from the past, we
should be thinking about this new drug culture. Although maybe not the way I was, half a century ago,
when I was thinking, "Wow! This is great f***ing s**t!"
(Notice that my thoughts were so fuzzy I was thinking
in asterisks.)

Recreational marijuana is now legal in ten states,
the District of Columbia, and the U.S. territory of the
Northern Mariana Islands (talk about "far out"). Two
countries—Canada and Uruguay (the Canada of Latin
America)—have fully legalized the consumption and
sale of marijuana. Two other countries (with absolutely
nothing else in common)—South Africa and the former
Soviet Republic of Georgia—have declared all personal
possession legal. Marijuana is legally tolerated in licensed
cafés in the Netherlands. At least thirty-two other nations, as diverse as Croatia and Jamaica and Luxembourg
and Ukraine, have decriminalized the drug.

Medical marijuana is legal in forty-eight countries
and in thirty-three U.S. states and all U.S. overseas ter-
ritories. We know how it goes with medical marijuana.
I have a great bumper sticker idea, yours free for the
taking.

MEDICAL MARIJUANA MAKES ME SICK!

Health care provider: "What are your symptoms?"
Patient: "I'm not getting high."

Marijuana has become . . . well, maybe not exactly "respectable" but no more worthy of rebuke than walking down Bourbon Street with a Hurricane in a Solo cup. (Although if you've got a doobie in your other hand you can still get ticketed in New Orleans, $40 for a first offense. But to put the social odium in perspective, it's a $50 fine if you smoke a Marlboro in a Bourbon Street bar.)

Marijuana is an accepted fact. And it's almost a fact that other mind-altering drugs will be accepted. (I love that phrase "mind-altering drugs." As if there were no changes in brain function after you drink six cups of coffee before doing your taxes or after you drink four martinis before putting the nut dish on your head, mounting the back of the sofa, and reciting "The Charge of the Light Brigade" to the cocktail party. But I digress. Which I find I'm doing a lot while writing about the drug culture. It may have something to do with the drugs. I'll have to go ask Alice, when she's ten feet tall.)

In 2014 *Scientific American* ran an editorial, "End the Ban on Psychoactive Drug Research."

In 2017 the National Institutes of Health publication *Neuropsychopharmacology* (take a big toke and say *that* without exhaling) presented a peer-reviewed paper, "Modern Clinical Research on LSD," supportive of the position taken in the *Scientific American* editorial. The paper noted, "Clinical research on LSD came to a halt in the early 1970s because of political pressure," said, "The first modern research findings from studies of LSD . . . have only very recently been published," and concluded, in its abstract, "These data should contribute to further investigations of the therapeutic potential of LSD in psychiatry."

In 2018 the *Journal of Palliative Medicine* published an article, "Taking Psychedelics Seriously," saying, "Recent published studies have demonstrated the safety and efficacy of psilocybin ['shrooms], MDMA [ecstasy], and ketamine [rave drug favorite Special K] when administered in a medically supervised and monitored approach."

Of course "palliative medicine" is the treatment of terminally ill patients so no jokes, please, about people "dying to get a hold of these drugs." But the path to legalization does seem to go through the doctor's office before it gets to *The Doors of Perception*, as Aldous Huxley called his serious, thoughtful, scholarly book about getting stoned.

Which is the point of drugs. Not that we sixties "heads" weren't "like, really into" serious, thoughtful, scholarly excuses for drug taking.

Back in 1902 William James, philosopher, physician, and "the father of American psychology," wrote in *The Varieties of Religious Experience*:

> Our normal waking consciousness . . . is but one special type of consciousness, whilst all about it, parted by the filmiest of screens, there lie potential forms of consciousness entirely different . . . No account of the universe in its totality can be final which leaves these forms of consciousness quite disregarded.

This was James's excuse for getting stoned on nitrous oxide. None of us heads had sat down and read *The Varieties of Religious Experience*. But we all knew about the laughing gas.

More contemporaneous to the 1960s, psychology PhD and former Harvard professor Timothy Leary was on the college lecture circuit advocating that we blow our minds: "These wondrous plants and drugs could free man's consciousness and bring a new conception of man, his psychology and philosophy."

I went to hear Leary speak when he came to my school and . . . I refer the reader back to the second paragraph of this chapter.

I got the Leary quote from an anthology of 1960s *Esquire* articles that was sitting on my bookshelf. In 1968 Leary wrote a piece for the magazine that starts out as an account of a 1960 psychedelic drug experiment supposedly for clinical research purposes supposedly conducted under controlled circumstances and ends with two naked beatnik poets—Allen Ginsberg and Peter Orlovsky—wandering around Leary's house while his teenage daughter is trying to do her homework.

Leary also spoke at my friend Dave Barry's school. Dave has a better recollection of the experience, which he recounts in his book *Dave Barry Turns 50*.

Naturally, being college students, we did not rush out and take a powerful, potentially harmful drug that we knew virtually nothing about just because some guy told us to. No sir. First we asked some hard questions, such as: "Where can we get some?" *Then* we rushed out and took it.

We participants in the sixties drug culture *did* want to open "the doors of perception." There is indeed a lot about life, the world, and the universe that we don't perceive in our ordinary day-to-day consciousness. And we could have perceived a lot more of it if we'd taken courses in biology, geology, chemistry, physics, and astronomy instead of getting wasted and spacing out on the slideshow in Art Appreciation 101. ("Darkness at Noon"—easy A. The doddering professor had been giving the same multiple-choice exam for forty-five years.)

We *were* searching for "cosmic truths." Although we weren't searching very hard, judging by the cosmic truths we found.

I am he as you are he as you are me
And we are all together

We were seeking "cosmic unity." One of the times when I took LSD I had just become one with the entire universe when the landlord knocked on the door of my off-campus apartment. The rent on the entire universe was two month overdue.

And we were looking for personal insights. For all I know I had some. But I don't believe they were any more profound than the lyrics in the previously cited Beatles song "I Am the Walrus." Which, many years of drug-free adult experience indicates, I am not. (Although I am tending more toward the 4,400-pound weight of a mature male *Odobenus rosmarus* than I was when I was nineteen, plus whiskers and, thanks to a partial plate and orthopedic shoes, tusks and flippers.)

Anyway, when it comes to self-analysis, drugs are a one-man birthday party. You don't get any presents you didn't bring.

Goo goo g'joob

But the sixties drug culture *did* produce some great music. Unless you've made the mistake of going back and listening to it. What did the Grateful Dead fan say when he ran out of pot? *What a shitty band!*

Turning on, tuning in, and dropping out unleashed a great wave of personal creativity—macramé plant hangers, posters for rock concerts at the Fillmore Auditorium with psychedelic lettering that was illegible unless you were too stoned to read, the cover art for the White Album, and hippie chick embroidery on jean jackets. These are comparable to the sculpture of Donatello, the illuminated manuscript of the Book of Kells, the painting of Caravaggio, and the couture of Coco Chanel. If you're on PCP.

So what *can* the twenty-first century learn from the drug culture of the 1960s? Again, I refer the reader to my second paragraph. While doing some background reading, however, I did come across one helpful hint, which might be especially useful to America's political class. In 2015 Cambridge University Press published a volume in its Cambridge Essential Histories series called *American Hippies*, by W. J. Rorabaugh, who quotes the Yale law professor and counterculture advocate Charles Reich, author of the 1970 bestselling panegyric to the 1960s, *The Greening of America.*

Says Reich, "No one can take himself seriously in bell-bottoms."

Can the Government
Be Run Like a Business?

"Government should be run like a business" is a bromide of long standing among fiscal conservatives, market-oriented libertarians, pragmatic liberals, and other people who think that politics and practicality ought to be a better match.

It should be noted that just because something is called a "bromide" doesn't mean it doesn't work. Potassium bromide is an effective sedative and anticonvulsant. It's no longer prescribed as a medicine, however, because of its high level of toxicity.

But that's much more than we know about the bromide of running government like a business, which has never been submitted to a meaningful trial.

We did elect a businessman to the presidency in 2016. But there's considerable evidence that he's not good at running businesses. Trump Taj Mahal, Trump Plaza Hotel, and Trump Entertainment Resorts all went bankrupt. He is good at branding. But branding a business is different from running one. Besides, "America" was already well established as a brand.

Very few American presidents have had significant business careers before they became president. I'm not counting the management of large plantations by early presidents such as Washington, Jefferson, Madison, and Jackson. We have a name for the slave labor business model. It's called evil.

And I'm not counting show business either. It's such an oddball enterprise that I'm not sure what lessons are to be learned from it. Okay maybe *The Apprentice* serves as an inspiration for Trump's cabinet meetings the way *Bedtime for Bonzo* served as an inspiration for Reagan's.

The few presidents we've had who were chief executives before they were *the* chief executive either didn't try or didn't get a chance to apply business methods to government matters.

An exception was Warren Harding, editor and publisher of a lucrative Ohio newspaper. Unfortunately Harding's business method was corruption.

Both presidents Bush did have pre-presidential business careers. Bush 41 had done reasonably well in oil exploration, but not so well that he ever earned the West Texas nickname "Gusher George."

As co-owner of the Texas Rangers, George W. Bush made over $14 million when the team was sold in 1998. But in 2010 the team was bought by Ray Davis and Bob Simpson for $593 million. Businesswise, Bush 43 seems to have left money on the table.

As president, however, each George faced challenges no CEO ever confronts. There isn't any MBA case study that prepares you for the Gulf War or 9/11.

And speaking of CEOs, it's interesting what happened when Donald Rumsfeld (ex-CEO of G. D. Searle pharmaceutical corporation) was handed the management of the Iraq War. The merger and acquisition went well but in the end the stockholders (U.S. occupying troops, Iraqi civilians, victims of ISIS terrorism) weren't gratified.

In fact, it's been ninety-two years since we elected a president who was a truly successful businessman. The brilliantly entrepreneurial Herbert Hoover was a mining engineer who became a multimillionaire silver, lead, and zinc magnate. (No wonder Hoover favored "hard money." Although, personally, I'm not sure I want a zinc-backed U.S. dollar.)

Alas, things did not work out well for "The Herbert"— 1929 stock market crash, Great Depression, etc.

To be fair, Hoover had been in office for less than eight months when economic disaster struck. It wasn't all his fault. Nonetheless, "Great Depression" is the feeling that comes over anybody who tries to look at the U.S. government as a business.

In the first place, the USG "corporation" is a monopoly. Do not try to start your own government. We settled the question of whether that's a good idea at Appomattox Court House in 1865.

And we settled it rightly. The former Yugoslavia gives us an example of what happens when a country—even a minor country—splits into lots of little countries.

When it comes to government one is enough. But that still leaves us with a monopoly situation.

Monopolies are infamous for charging high prices in return for shoddy goods and services. USG is true to form. We pay the high prices on April 15 and we see the shoddy goods and services in—to name just two examples—the nation's infrastructure and our VA hospitals.

But aren't monopolies also infamous for reaping huge profits? The USG balance sheet is projected to show a loss of $1.08 trillion in 2020 and has been in the red for forty-six of the past fifty years.

USG is a terrible monopolist. Government is like a kid playing a game of Monopoly. The kid has hotels (in government it's called "eminent domain") on Boardwalk and Park Place and on all green, yellow, red, and orange properties. The kid owns (by way of the Departments of Transportation and Energy) the railroads and the utilities. And the kid has a "Get Out of Jail Free" card. (Note present and past presidential pardons.) Then what does the kid do? Spills an alphabet soup of federal regulatory agencies on the board; stomps on the top hat, wheelbarrow, race car, and Scottie dog tokens of free enterprise, and takes all the Federal Reserve Bank Monopoly Money and throws it out the playroom window.

No amount of entrepreneurial savvy can fix this game. The playroom's been a mess since 1776. And no business wizard can spank the kid. The kid is the American public.

"Can government be run like a business?" Yes—a bad one.

Two, Four, Six, Eight
Who Do We Appreciate . . .
The Electoral College!

As we all learned in our civics class . . . or would have if we hadn't been staring out the window, napping, or drawing toupees on pictures of President Eisenhower in the textbook . . . in an American presidential election voters actually do not vote for a presidential candidate. They vote for an "elector" who is pledged to vote for that candidate.

As per rules set down in the U.S. Constitution, the president of the United States is elected by an institution called the Electoral College.

The way this works—in simple terms, to keep us awake and not looking for photos of Ike to deface— is that each state gets electors in the Electoral College equal to the state's number of congressional districts plus two (its number of senators). And the District of Columbia also gets three electors (because back in 1961 the residents of Washington, D.C., complained that they weren't getting a say about the president even though the whole city is filled with people who won't shut up about the president).

Thus the Electoral College has 538 electors. The presidential candidate who receives the majority of their votes becomes president.

Choosing electors in each state is mostly a matter of winner-take-all. The presidential candidate with the most votes in a state gets that state's votes in the Electoral College. (Maine and Nebraska can split their electors according to who wins in which congressional district—but we'll let the lobster mongers and corn shuckers worry about that.)

There is such a thing as a "faithless elector," who doesn't vote for the candidate to whom he or she is pledged. In the 2016 Electoral College proceedings Colin Powell received three votes and John Kasich, Ron Paul, Faith Spotted Eagle, and Bernie Sanders received one each.

Being a faithless elector is like committing adultery—against the law in some states and not in others. But, as with adultery, arrest and prosecution are rare. And in the history of American presidential elections Electoral College faithlessness has never led to any change in who became president (or, so far as we know, who slept around with Bernie Sanders).

The Electoral College is complex but its effect is simple: it gives the parts of America where people are thin on the ground greater say over who's president than they'd have if only thick people were counted.

Before we discuss whether this is a good thing or a bad thing, first let's *not* discuss the 2016 presidential election.

While it's true that a certain person—who has insisted on constantly, repeatedly reminding us—won the "popular vote" (or not quite, since she got 48.2 percent), it's also true that she was, as it were, *trumped* by another person in the Electoral College, 304 to 227.

But. The two of them knew the rules and campaigned accordingly. If they had been running to gain a majority of the popular vote instead of a majority of the Electoral College vote they would have conducted different campaigns.

Worse campaigns. Campaigns aimed at the lowest common denominator of voters—at the hoi polloi, the masses, the mob. Political thinkers have theorized that mob rule would create a society marked by selfishness, stupidity, instability, and a vicious tendency to scapegoat. Political thinkers can quit theorizing. Behold Facebook, Twitter, YouTube, Instagram, Snapchat, Tumblr, Reddit, WhatsApp, WhosApp, WheresApp, WhensApp, etc.

The 2016 presidential campaign was ugly but could have been uglier if both candidates had put even more emphasis on vulgar rabble-rousing and vast gatherings of fanatical adherents.

Picture, on the one hand, a gigantic Nuremberg Nerd Rally, camera ready for a lefty Leni Riefenstahl's *Triumph of the Hillary*. And, on the other, a Red State Square with a parade of ballistic Trumps rolling through it, reviewed by a Trump Politburo atop Trump's Tomb on Trump Day.

Right, there are two good reasons to keep the Electrical College. It forces our presidential candidates out into the boonies to be dragged from their private jets and comfy campaign buses at all hours and stuffed with starchy waffle mix at Rotary pancake breakfasts, smeared with canned tomato sauce at volunteer fire department spaghetti dinners, queried about local zoning ordinances by yokels in town halls, picketed (or endorsed) by special interests so special that no one has any interest in them, and otherwise made to behave like the small and inconsequential personages that our presidential candidates are.

We may—and we do—elect fools, but at least we elected them out in the open where we can see what they're doing.

But what's more important about the Electoral College is that it gives a vote not only to Americans but to America itself. We give weight in our political system to *place* as well as to *people*.

The population of Alaska, Montana, North Dakota, South Dakota, and Wyoming combined is less than the population of the San Francisco metropolitan area (and—bonus—doesn't include a single person who lives in San Francisco).

Under a system of "direct" election by popular vote this would leave 1,058,000 square miles of America with less influence over who becomes president than 14.4 square inches of the iPhone invented by San Francisco native Steve Jobs, and he's dead.

Steve Jobs liked to pay lip service to the "environment." So do the people of the San Francisco metropolitan area.

And yet when it comes to allowing that environment to have any voice in national politics . . .

According to the Census Bureau, 62.7 percent of Americans live in urban areas, on only 3.5 percent of the country's land. They don't live in the American environment, they live indoors in the American "in-vironment."

I'm concerned about the safety and well-being of these people. City folks do go outdoors. But they go outdoors only in order to annoy the place—with their overly revealing bathing suits, skimpy shorts in all seasons, rattletrap mountain bikes, smelly hiking boots, unwieldy backpacks, ugly running shoes, overpriced skis, dim bulb surfer slag, and noisy skateboard antics.

This is why city folks are so often painfully sunburned, afflicted with hypothermia, chased by cougars, eaten by bears, medivaced from nature reserves, bitten by snakes, buried in avalanches, attacked by sharks, and hit by cars.

It's interesting how rarely these things happen to people who work and live outdoors. Perhaps that's because they've been to Electoral College.

Is a Reasonable, Sensible, Moderate Foreign Policy Even Possible?

As I've mentioned, I consider myself to be a libertarian—to a reasonable, sensible, moderate degree. That is, I believe in individual freedom, individual dignity, and individual responsibility as long as I get to be an irresponsible undignified freeloader at least every so often.

Anyway, as a person who subscribes to the principles of libertarianism somewhat, I have somewhat of a problem with foreign policy. Libertarian philosophy is based on free individuals. Many of the world's individuals aren't free and, in foreign policy terms, none of us are individuals. We're little bits and pieces of a nation.

Nations can't be regarded in the same way as individuals. Nations don't have equal rights before the law because . . . there is no law. (Oh, supposedly, there's such a thing as "international law," but really? Nice try, world court in The Hague.)

Foreign policy is ruled by force. Matthew 11:12, "The kingdom of heaven suffereth violence, and the violent bear it away."

Foreign policy is never an individual enterprise. "*I'm going to invade Ukraine*" is a harmless statement—at most a plea for help from mental health professionals. "*Russia* is going to invade Ukraine" is a different kind of statement, especially if it's made by the Kremlin.

Foreign policy is always a collective enterprise. Even the freest nations bind their citizens into collective enterprises, particularly when it comes to international relations. In fact international relations are worse than actual relations. As Grandfather O'Rourke said to me, "I don't care if all the kids next door won Nobel Peace Prizes and all your cousins are in jail, *family is family*."

Collective enterprise undercuts individual enterprise. Inside a free nation, individual interests are balanced through democracy and rule of law. Therefore individual enterprise can be assumed to be—over the long term, on average, in aggregate—rational.

Collective enterprise can be assumed to be no such thing. The interests of collective enterprises, such as foreign policy, have no balancing mechanism with the interests of other collective enterprises, such as foreigners' foreign policy.

Collective enterprises may be inert and benign like coral reefs. But even then they're thoughtless and lack individual freedom and dignity.

When humans are involved, collective enterprises are more often busy and active and fraught with potential for, at best, amoral conduct and, at worst, outright evils such as dictatorship, oligarchy, or mob rule.

The dictators and oligarchs might be, individually, nice enough people. (I have it on good authority that even Bashar al-Assad is personable around the house.) But they *will* give in to the temptations of their collective power. And collective power, unlike individual freedom, is not constrained by reason. Likewise mob rule is extremely dangerous no matter whether the mob is wearing slogan T-shirts and carrying hand-lettered placards or wearing bedsheets and carrying flaming crosses.

In other words, collective enterprises suck, and foreign policy is one.

This is the problem. What's the solution? We've tried having no foreign policy at all. Pearl Harbor. Isolationism didn't work. We've tried aggressive internationalism. Vietnam. Didn't work. We've tried apologizing for our aggressive internationalism. Obama. Arab Spring. Didn't work. We've tried sanctions. Putin persists. Kim Jong-un endures. Ayatollah Khamenei abides. Didn't work. And we've tried electing a loudmouth commander in chief and having him go CAPS LOCK on Twitter . . .

Probably there's no such thing as a foreign policy that "works" in the sense of making problems with foreigners go away. It's like an endless road trip with kids in the backseat of the car. Sooner or later we're going to have to turn around and say, "Don't make me come back there!"

So let's limit the consideration of foreign policy to America's use of military force. That's the crux of the matter, the realpolitik equivalent of parents who spank.

Use of military force is definitionally a collective enterprise. And it's the part of foreign policy that's much more dangerous than, for example, trade agreements. I'd rather pay lots for high tariff goods at Target than shoot people, not to mention have them shooting back.

One of the clearest thinkers about American use of military force is former national security adviser, former chairman of the Joint Chiefs of Staff, and former secretary of state Colin Powell.

General Powell was chairman of the Joint Chiefs during the Gulf War. (Did work.) He proposed eight questions that should be answered "yes" before America uses military force. These became known as the Powell Doctrine.

Let's apply the Powell Doctrine to a current foreign policy issue. Not a grave, portentous geopolitical foreign policy issue like the Middle East. That's too complicated. We'd be here (like the Middle East has been there) for thousands of years. Let's apply the Powell Doctrine to a less sweeping foreign policy issue closer to home: illegal immigration.

The United States has deployed more than six thousand troops on the Mexican–American border to stop illegal immigration. Put that to the Powell Doctrine test.

1. **Is a vital national security interest threatened?**
   Well, ragtag bands of Guatemalans, Salvadorans, and unemployed campesinos hardly make for a *Red Dawn* scenario. And, say what you will against

illegal immigrants, their cuisine is a lot better than the commies'.

2. **Do we have a clear attainable objective?** No immigrants at all? I'd be digging potatoes in County Mayo.

3. **Have the risks and costs been fully and frankly analyzed?** Mexico, I've been told, is paying for the costs of the wall, but there seems to be some risk that the check will get lost in the mail.

4. **Have all other nonviolent policy means been fully exhausted?** There are 16,600 (reasonably) nonviolent border patrol agents assigned to the region, and they *are* exhausted. But if we gave them some energy drinks to keep them up all night they could stand in a line along the two-thousand-mile international boundary and be only about 600 feet apart. Or we could reform our immigration process so that applicants for residency got a quick, clear answer without arrest, detention, and years of bureaucratic wrangling.

5. **Is there a plausible exit strategy to avoid endless entanglement?** Other than conquering Mexico? We tried that already. Of course, if we'd left well enough alone in 1846 the people now trying to sneak across our border would be Californians. Frankly, I'd rather have the people we're getting.

6. **Have the consequences of our action been fully considered?** No. If it weren't for illegal immigrants I couldn't find *anybody* to mow my lawn.

7. **Is the action supported by the American people?**
   In the "paid for" sense of supported? Considering
   our deficit and national debt, Americans aren't *supporting* anything these days.

8. **Do we have genuine broad international support?** Ha! Our strongest international supporters
   are busy trying to get into America illegally.

Of course no doctrine is perfect. Powell himself inad-
vertently violated the Powell Doctrine—if unwittingly—
when, as secretary of state, basing his decision on
imperfect and distorted intelligence reports, he coun-
tenanced the Iraq War. (Didn't work.)

But at least General Powell devised a rational means
of thinking about a collective enterprise with an individual mind.

If we applied the Powell Doctrine rigorously to American foreign policy, I wonder how many things we'd find
that are even more absurd and perilous than deploying
the military to the middle of nowhere to prevent my
lawn from being mowed?

On a Personal Note . . .

Colin Powell is a man I respect and admire.
And I really like him too, even though I've met
him only a few times.

I interviewed him in the early 2000s when I
was working for the *Atlantic* and he was secretary
of state. The *Atlantic* is a magazine that takes

itself very seriously, something Secretary Powell does not. (He tells a great story about the relentless tendency of government to *govern*, no matter what. Shortly after he'd retired he had his initial encounter with private life air travel. He bought a first-class one-way airline ticket to New York City, at the airline ticket counter, with cash, and without a reservation. As a result, at the security checkpoint, he got a full body search and complete luggage dissection—from TSA agents *who recognized him*. "Hi, Secretary Powell! We'll be done here in a moment, sir!")

My interview—the *Atlantic* being the *Atlantic*—was supposed to be very serious, probably about the Powell Doctrine or something. But Secretary Powell likes cars and so do I, and we spent the hour in his vast, trappings-of-power secretary of state office talking about cars.

Powell is a fan of old Volvos. And my *Atlantic* editors were not wildly pleased when I came back with an hour-long tape-recorded on-the-record discussion of Volvo PV544s, 122s, 140s, 164s, and P1800 Ghia-bodied sport coupes.

But I thought it was valuable information. Old Volvos are an important element in certain vital security issues, such as your kids starting to drive.

Years later, when my eldest daughter turned sixteen, I got her an old Volvo—a 2007 XC70 with a hundred thousand miles on it. Of course—sixteen-year-olds being sixteen-year-olds—she had an accident. She was driving down a back road with a Toyota ahead of her and a Honda behind. A deer ran in front of the Toyota whose driver slammed on the brakes. My daughter rear-ended the Toyota, and the Honda rear-ended my daughter. The Toyota's trunk was bashed in almost to the rear window. The Honda's hood was crumpled up to the windshield. The Volvo? A broken taillight.

My eldest daughter is now off at college. Her younger sister is driving the XC70. And she's about to pass it down to her kid brother.

Thank you, Colin Powell, for more than just the Powell Doctrine.

The Inaugural Address I'd Like To Hear the President—Whoever It May Be—Deliver

On January 20, 2021, the president of the United States will give his or her inaugural address.

If that president is Donald Trump, we already know this is not the kind of thing he's any good at. And none of the prospective Democratic candidates are riveting public speakers either. But it's a low bar. Most presidential inaugural addresses are bad.

There've been a few exceptions. Lincoln's second inaugural address was a masterpiece of soaring rhetoric. "With malice toward none; with charity for all; with firmness in the right, as God gives us to see the right."

Washington's second inaugural was a model of how all elected officials should speak. Which is briefly. His speech was 135 words long.

Most other inaugural addresses weren't memorable. Or, if we do remember them, they don't stand up to scrutiny.

FDR said, "The only thing we have to fear is fear itself." What does that even mean? A more reasonable statement at the time of Roosevelt's inauguration in 1933 would have been, "We have nothing to fear except being broke, out of a job, shoeless, hungry, and having the bank foreclose on our mortgage."

If we hadn't been afraid of all those things, FDR never would have gotten elected.

JFK said, "Ask not what your country can do for you, ask what you can do for your country." That's worse than nonsensical, it's wrong. National service may be an obligation during periods of extreme crisis. But the early 1960s wasn't one—until Kennedy made it so by bungling the Cuban missile crisis. Nations exist to serve people. People do not exist to serve nations.

So I won't listen to the inaugural address. I mean, I'll watch it on TV. Like any good reporter I've got to at least pretend to keep my eye on current events, especially in case the event is Trump getting reinaugurated and he cuts an enormous word fart or Chief Justice Roberts uses the Bible to swat him instead of swear him in. But otherwise I won't really be paying attention.

Instead, I'll be polishing an alternative speech, an inaugural address I'd *like* to hear a president deliver.

It will go something like this.

My fellow Americans. I want to thank the people who voted for me. I also want to thank the people who voted against me. Democracy is meaningless if it doesn't result from a meaningful competition be-tween ideas—the way the college football National Championship would have been meaningless if the top-ranked college team had played the tailgaters in the Hard Rock Stadium parking lot.

Furthermore, I want to thank the people who didn't vote. There's no shame in not voting. In fact, if a voter is unfamiliar with the issues and uniformed about the candidates, not voting is the right thing to do. It's a wise person who admits his or her ignorance. Over the next four years I promise that I frequently will be admitting my ignorance to you.

Also, a person who doesn't vote is reminding us all that there's a lot more more to America than its government.

And there's more to America's government than the person who's the head of it. In fact, it may be that America has been giving too much power and privilege to the person who is the head of its government.

I'm the new president. But I am only an individual. And we are a nation of laws, not men and women.

Because we are a country guided by rules instead of by personalities, I've been reading the rule book. I've been studying the Constitution of the United States of America.

I intend to play by the rules. I'm the president, but you the people own this country. You are the stockholders. Your elected representatives in Congress are the board of directors. And the chairman of the board is, again, you the people. I just work here.

In the Constitution, the president of the United States isn't even mentioned until Section 3 of Article I. And the only reason that he's mentioned there is to explain how Congress can impeach him.

Actually, the vice president is mentioned before the president is. That's because the vice president holds the office of president of the Senate where he has a tie-breaking vote.

Article I, Section 1, of the Constitution says, "All legislative Powers herein granted shall be vested in a Congress of the United States." To judge by that, our Founding Fathers were more concerned with what goes on in the House and the Senate than what goes on in the White House. Which, incidentally, they didn't bother to build until 1800.

The Constitution doesn't get around to listing the powers of the president until Article II, Sections 2 and 3, and the list is only four paragraphs long.

I'm commander in chief of the military. But in Article I, Section 8, the Constitution says Congress has the power to "declare War," to "make Rules concerning Captures on Land and Water" and to "raise and support Armies." So I guess what "commander in chief" really means is that, when the marines yell "Gung ho!" and charge, I'm supposed to go first.

I'm not looking forward to this part of the job because I'm a little concerned that the huge Secret Service motorcade with all the flashing blue lights that follows me everywhere I go will attract enemy fire.

Some people think the president is in charge of America's foreign policy. I don't know where they got that idea.

Yes, I'm allowed to make treaties but only "by and with the Advice and Consent of the Senate." And two-thirds of the Senate has to agree to the treaty. Two-thirds of the Senate can't agree on what they had for lunch in the Senate dining room.

And notice that while the Senate has the "consent" thing covered—senators love to vote on stuff—they tend to come up short on the "advice" part. The only advice a president gets from a senator is, "You should help me raise funds for my reelection campaign."

By the way, if you'd like a little advice and consent of my own, I'd advise you to consent to be more careful about who you elect to the Senate and the House of Representatives. We've got some real nut buckets up on Capitol Hill.

Anyway, as I was saying, I also get to appoint my ambassadors, my cabinet, and, when the occasion arises, Supreme Court justices. Unless, of course, the Senate advises me that they won't consent.

I have the "Power to grant Reprieves and Pardons for Offenses against the United States." Although, by custom, my major campaign donors won't get out of jail until the very end of my second term.

But I can fix my teenage son's speeding tickets—if he's careful to do his speeding only inside the

District of Columbia and not go over to Virginia and get arrested for speeding under a state law.

However, that huge Secret Service motorcade usually has traffic tied up in the District. So I'm afraid the kid won't get much of a chance to speed.

Mostly what I'm supposed to do as president is, according to the Constitution, "take Care that the laws be faithfully executed." I'm the national hall monitor.

The rest is paperwork. I can "require the Opinion, in writing, of the principal Officer in each of the executive Departments, upon any Subject relating to the Duties of their respective Offices."

And, under the Freedom of Information Act, so can the *New York Times*. A fat lot of good it does either of us.

Now let's all go have some fun at the inaugural balls. I'm going to attend all of them and have a few drinks at each. If I wake up late tomorrow with a bad headache and don't feel like working, don't worry. My job isn't all that important.

My Own Personal Fantasy League Presidential Election

Being, more or less, seated and clothed and in my right mind, I'm very unhappy with this presidential election. And there's nothing I can do about it. So I'm going to give up and retreat into a fantasy life.

No matter how bad reality is you can always use your imagination. You can wish upon a star for hope and change. (Or did somebody try that already?)

Anyway, come with me to the Land of Make-Believe. Let's pretend that a good, respectable, intelligent, decent, honest, and reasonable Democrat is running for president against a good, respectable, intelligent, decent, honest, and reasonable Republican.

Quit laughing. We're trying to have a daydream here.

As long as we're dreaming let's make the Democrat a working-class guy from the rust belt, a skilled machinist for instance, who runs a small business, has to make payroll, and feels the full effects of OSHA, EPA, EEOC, Obamacare, and every other government regulatory requirement.

And—since we're talking unicorns, flying ponies, and candy-flavored rainbows—let's make the Republican a woman from a disadvantaged minority background.

I've got nothing against GOP presidential candidates being random old white males. I'm one of those myself. But it's about time that Republicans heard from somebody—other than a Supreme Court justice or a former governor of Alaska—who knows what it feels like to be an excluded conservative outsider.

Given the direction that America's factionalized society, partisan animosities, and identity politics are headed, *everybody* is going to be feeling like an excluded outsider soon. The GOP should get with the program.

But I'm talking about reality again, and I promised not to do that. Let's get back to our castle in the air.

Suppose we've got these two ideal candidates. And suppose they debate each other. Do you think their debate would sound anything like the debates we've heard this year? That wouldn't be a dream. That would be a nightmare.

In our imaginary perfect world there wouldn't even be a debate moderator. (As far as I can tell the only reason we've had moderators in the real world debates is to bring the average IQ in the debate venue up to three figures.)

Our ideal candidates flip a coin to see who goes first, speak briefly, listen to what the other candidate says, respond to it, and don't interrupt.

Our Republican wins the toss.

Good Republican: "The most important issues facing our nation are the federal debt and deficit. When you find yourself down in a hole, quit digging. If we don't get government overspending under control we will end up with the soaring cost-price index and plunging economy of the "stagflation" we had in the 1970s and—heaven forbid—disco may make a comeback.

Good Democrat: I agree with my esteemed opponent about the dangers of the debt and deficit—and disco. But America has been down in this debt and deficit hole before, after World War II and after the Civil War. In both cases rapid economic growth was our ladder out. I believe the most important issue facing our nation is economic growth. I believe government has a role to play in stimulating growth through wise spending on much-needed infrastructure. And I mean *wise* spending —not sticking Solyndra solar panels where the sun never shines or building light rail to get stoned millennials back to their shared housing in downtown Portland.

GR: Yes, fixing the debt and deficit without economic growth would be like trout fishing in Death Valley. I'd stimulate the economy by cutting taxes and reduce the deficit by cutting spending. We know cutting taxes stimulates the economy. It's so obvious even a Death Valley dead trout would understand. Having more money makes you richer. As for spending, the U.S. GDP is about $19 trillion. Combined U.S. federal, state, and local government spending is about $6.5 trillion. That's almost a third of GDP. Oughta be enough! If you were sending a check for a third of your income every month to your stoned millennial kid in Portland, he could Uber.

GD: Fortunately, my millennial kid works in the family machine shop back in Cleveland and limits himself to a couple of beers on the weekend. However, I take your point. Unfortunately, about two-thirds of the federal budget goes to entitlement programs. And politicians from both parties have been about as willing and able as your dead trout to tackle entitlement cuts. I'd be a big liar if I said I had a quick fix for entitlement spending, even if I win majority support in the House and the Senate. Also, let us not forget that while entitlements can be—and are—abused, they also provide a lot of help to people who would be helpless without them. For example, Social Security, for all its problems, virtually eliminated severe poverty among the aged in America. Let's be honest here, do you really want your mother-in-law living in your spare bedroom until she's 103?

GR: You met my mother-in-law when our families went to church together. No.

GD: I also take your point about taxes, they are too high for some people. But then again, for some other people, maybe they're not high enough. While we're being honest, let me point out that I'm a Democrat. I *will* raise taxes on very rich people. Even Adam Smith, of whom you Republicans are so fond, had something to say in favor of a graduated income tax. Smith pointed out that one of the principle duties of government is to protect property. People with a lot of property should pay a higher *rate* of taxation because they get a higher *rate* of protection. Paying taxes is like paying for a guard dog. But, if you don't have anything to guard, all you're paying for is a stray pit bull.

GR: We'll have to agree to disagree about rates of taxation. But you must admit our tax *system* is a mess. The U.S. tax code is now four million words long. If you printed that out and dropped it on a taxpayer it would squash him flat.

GD: Yeah, he'd be road kill. You could peel him off the highway and sail him like a Frisbee.

GR: We've got to do something about that.

GD: We sure do. I've got some specific ideas about how to do it.

GR: So do I. Let's discuss them.

And the debate would continue in just such a manner—substantive but good-natured—for exactly one hour.

Because, no matter how good presidential candidates are, an hour of listening to them is all we can stand, even in our dreams.

At the end of the debate the Good Republican would say to the Good Democrat, "You obviously care about people. If I'm elected I'm going to appoint you secretary of health and human services—and of education too, because, to save money, I'm gong to eliminate that cabinet post and put it back into the Department of Health, Education, and Welfare."

The Good Democrat would say to the Good Republican, "You're obviously sharp about fiscal and monetary policy. If I'm elected I'm going to appoint you secretary of the Treasury."

And then they'd hug.

Now I'll wake up and wipe the drool off my face.

A License to Drive
(Me Crazy)

We should license politicians. Every other profession has some form of accreditation or certification. There are hundreds, possibly thousands, of politicians in Washington, none with any formal qualifications for the job. Yet in the District of Columbia more than 125 other occupations require a license.

We license lawyers, doctors, teachers, accountants, plumbers, real estate brokers, marriage counselors, dental hygienists, cosmetologists, beauticians, and barbers. But a politician has the power to cause more damage and expense than even the worst hair stylist.

As the behavior of lawyers in Washington law firms shows, licensing is no cure-all. Most politicians are lousy. A license to practice won't make them better. But creating complicated and time-consuming regulatory barriers to becoming a politician might, at least, limit the number of louses.

Politicians should be rigorously educated and highly trained. At college they need to study subjects pertinent to their field. Just eight semesters of abnormal psych may not be enough.

But let's not send them to our best schools such as Georgetown, Yale, Columbia, or Penn. We've tried this before, with mixed results. Is Trump University still open?

Perhaps future politicians should study political science. Ha. Ha. Ha. No. If politics were a science it would have been tried on lab rats first.

More important are the academic disciplines that proto-politicos need to *avoid*.

Mathematics One look at the federal budget would make a mathematician's head explode.

Logic Putting a logical person in politics is like putting an astrologer in charge of the Hubble Space Telescope.

Literature and English Composition Have you read the memoirs by successful politicians after they've left office? They didn't achieve preeminence by knowing how to recognize literary skills in a ghost writer.

The most promising candidates in the making will concentrate on campus social life, especially in the dining hall. A vital skill in running for office—especially during presidential primaries—is, as previously noted, the ability to eat six pancake breakfasts and five spaghetti dinners a day at town halls, volunteer fire departments, VFW Posts, Elks Lodges, the Junior Chamber of Commerce, Rotary, Kiwanis, Lions Clubs, American Legion, Knights of Columbus, and B'nai B'rith.

Between meals students can gain additional experience in practical politics by standing on a chair and reciting the same twenty-minute piece of rote gibberish over and over, then taking questions from classmates. (One of which is sure to be "Why don't you sit down and shut up?"—an existential query that anyone who wants to be a politician ought to ponder deeply.)

And the advantages of the fraternity and sorority system should not be neglected. Some day a secret handshake (or an embarrassing pledge stunt photo, especially if the pledge happens to be in a fraternity or sorority other than one's own) could be worth millions in campaign fund-raising.

Still one shudders to think what a "political" Animal House would be like—"Toga! Toga! Toga!" Except practicing with real knives, to be a real Brutus, in a real Senate.

On the other hand, political students should avoid student politics. Student politics consist of either donning black ski masks and chasing guest lecturers off campus or tying bow ties and finding pairs of George Will horn-rims to wear to Young Americans for Freedom meetings. This is excellent training to be a lousy voter. But the point is to be a lousy politician.

We have a long history of lousy politicians in this country. America wouldn't be the nation that it is today without the likes of—to name just a few—Aaron Burr, Millard Fillmore, Warren Harding, Huey Long, Richard Nixon, and James Michael Curley (who served as mayor of Boston while in a federal penitentiary).

We need a rigorous test to ensure that our politicians meet (but do not exceed) America's traditional standards of lousiness. It should be something like a bar exam or, maybe, in this case, a "low bar" exam.

There would be an essay question. "Say nothing of substance in 5,000 words or more. Extra credit for saying less at greater length."

And a fill-in-the-blanks section.

Define the Following

Boodle _____

Graft _____

Jobbery _____

Pork Barrel _____

Gerrymander _____

Logrolling _____

Carpetbagging _____

Wire-Pulling _____

Gravy Train _____

And multiple choice.

Circle the Correct Answer

A. The gloves are off in this election.

B. I will do what it takes to win.

C. Really. I mean it. Bring on the dark money. Unleash the scare ads. Hello, foreign troll farms. I promise every American a $50-an-hour minimum wage and a free service animal.

D. All of the above.

There will be no true/false section in the test, however. True and false are simply not political concepts. It will have to be a false/false test instead.

"I will bring new ideas to Washington."

☐ False   ☐ False

"I look forward to building bipartisan support for my programs."

☐ False   ☐ False

"I didn't do it."

☐ False   ☐ False

"And I'll never do it again."

☐ False   ☐ False

"I have the full support of my loving spouse and family."

☐ False   ☐ False

The Founding Fathers
Have Some Words With Us

Our partisan political conflict has turned into the kind of ugly, brutal, and merciless persecution that filled the Roman Colosseum during the time of the emperor Nero, but where are the Christians? We have a murderous spectacle where vicious, bloodthirsty wild animals roam the arena in Washington. However, none of their victims are faithful, innocent, brave, or good.

Let us turn away our eyes from this unholy gore and look instead for some wisdom and advice from our Founding Fathers.

The Founders were not, of course, invariably wise advisers. They could be silly. Thomas Jefferson predicted "there is not a *young man* now living in the United States who will not die a Unitarian."* (Current membership of American Unitarian Universalist congregations: 154,704.)

And the Founders could be wrong. After James Madison had served in the Virginia legislature he wrote a

---

* Letter to Benjamin Waterhouse, the first doctor to employ smallpox vaccine in America thereby keeping a number of young men alive long enough to become Methodists, Baptists, and so forth.

1787 memorandum, "Vices of the Political System of the United States," expressing shock at the pork-barreling, logrolling, horse-trading nature of practical politics. As if practical politics ever had any other nature.

John Adams argued, "The law . . . will not bend to the uncertain wishes, imaginations, and wanton tempers of men."* Yes it will.

In fact, the Founders could be very wrong indeed. Alexander Hamilton, in *Federalist* no. 84, dismissed the need for a Bill of Rights.**

Jefferson, in his 1785 *Notes on the State of Virginia*, said, "Those who labor in the earth are the chosen people of God"—a statement that would have surprised the slaves who labored in the earth on Jefferson's plantation. And to whom did Jefferson expect to sell the fruits of this earth? He was always ready to insult those who engaged in trade. "Merchants have no country," he wrote in a letter to an admiring colleague,*** going on to impugn the patriotism merchants feel for "the mere spot they

---

* Adams was, of all things, acting as defense attorney in the murder trial of British soldiers who had fired into an angry Patriot mob during the 1770 Boston Massacre. Although Adams was a prominent opponent of British rule he felt morally obligated to ensure that the soldiers received a fair trail. (Also, he detested mobs, patriotic or otherwise.)
** Hamilton believed these rights were already protected under common law and that if a federal government were allowed to meddle in common law the meddling would never cease. (Which it hasn't, but God knows what kind of meddling the federal government would have gotten up to if we *didn't* have a Bill of Rights.)
*** Horatio G. Spafford, author of the 1824 *Gazetteer of the State of New York*, who, given the mercantile basis of New York's economy, should have told Jefferson to put a sock in it.

stand on" compared to the spot "from which they draw their gains." No wonder Jefferson died deeply in debt to a whole bunch of merchants.

But the Founders did possess sound good sense about intransigent political ideology and rabid political partisanship. They're crap.

Being men of the eighteenth-century Enlightenment, the Founders put their thoughts more eloquently. But Benjamin Franklin was almost that blunt about the dangers of falling in love with one's own opinions and deciding to be the smartest person in the room (especially after everyone else has left). And George Washington, on the subject of party politics, sounds like he's one fuck short of a fuck you.

Below is what they had to say.

On the last day of the Constitutional Convention, September 17, 1787, Benjamin Franklin was concerned that too many delegates would be unwilling to sign a Constitution that had resulted from so much—often strongly disputed —compromise. He wanted to make a short speech urging the Constitution's adoption. Franklin was too weak and ill to give the speech himself. It was delivered on his behalf by fellow Pennsylvania delegate James Wilson and recorded in James Madison's notes on the convention. (Which, one trusts, were more coherent than the notes I took in Government 101: *How a Bill becomes a Law— Cong. propose markup something something subcommittee something vote conference vote veto or something.*)

Franklin's speech is concise—by the standards of the day. It's worth salving our itchy little modern attention span to read the text in full. Besides, Franklin was one of the few, if not the only, Founder to publicly display a sense of humor. (Although Founding Mother Abigail Adams was good at privately teasing her self-serious husband, John: "Whilst you are proclaiming peace and good will to men, emancipating all nations, you insist upon retaining an absolute power over wives."*)

Benjamin Franklin

Mr. President [Franklin was formally addressing the Constitutional Convention's president, who happened to be our other admonitory Founding Father George Washington], I confess that there are several parts of this constitution which I do not at present approve [Franklin, wisely, did not list them, though he preferred a unicameral legislature and thought the chief executive had too much power and should be replaced by a committee, etc.], but I am not sure I shall never approve them: For having lived long, I have experienced many instances of being obliged by better information, or fuller consideration, to change opinions even on important subjects which I once thought right, but found to be otherwise. It is therefore that the older I grow, the more apt I am to doubt my own judgment, and to pay more respect to the judgment of others.

---

* From a 1776 letter to that husband.

Most men indeed as well as most sects in Religion, think themselves in possession of all truth, and that wherever others differ from them it is so far error. Steele* a Protestant in a Dedication tells the Pope, that the only difference between our Churches in their opinions of the certainty of their doctrines is, the Church of Rome is infallible and the Church of England is never in the wrong. But though many private persons think almost as highly of their own infallibility as of that of their sect, few express it so naturally as a certain french lady, who in a dispute with her sister, said "I don't know how it happens, Sister but I meet with no body but myself, that's always in the right—*Il n'y a que moi qui a toujours raison.***"

In these sentiments, Sir, I agree to this Constitution with all its faults, if they are such; [and, given the "three fifths of all other Persons" clause of Article I, Section 2, they were such, as Franklin, an ex–slave owner who had become an abolitionist, well knew] because I think a general Government necessary for us, and there is no form of Government but what may be a blessing to the people if well administered, and believe farther that this is likely to be well administered for a course of years [twenty-five years to

---

* Richard Steele, playwright and essayist, founded the British magazine *The Spectator* with Joseph Addison in 1711. The magazine was popular in the American colonies. Steele was a stern moralist—and, as Franklin's audience knew, a duelist, drinking man, and father of an illegitimate child. Thus Steele's name itself was a laugh line.
** "There's no one who is always right but me."

be exact, until the stupid War of 1812], and can only
end in Despotism, as other forms have done before it,
when the people shall become so corrupted as to need
despotic Government, being incapable of any other.
[One shudders to think what Franklin's opinion of
the election of 2020 would be.] I doubt too whether
any other Convention we can obtain, may be able to
make a better Constitution. For when you assemble
a number of men to have the advantage of their joint
wisdom, you inevitably assemble with those men, all
their prejudices, their passions, their errors of opinion, their local interests, and their selfish views. [Lie
down with dogs, get up with fleas.] From such an
assembly can a perfect production be expected? [Irony
is not a twenty-first-century invention.] It therefore
astonishes me, Sir, to find this system approaching so
near to perfection as it does; and I think it will aston-
ish our enemies, who are waiting with confidence to
hear that our councils are confounded like those of
the Builders of Babel; and that our States are on the
point of separation, only to meet hereafter for the
purpose of cutting one another's throats. [Which we
would do in 1861.]

Thus I consent, Sir, to this Constitution because
I expect no better, and because I am not sure, that it
is not the best. The opinions I have had of its errors,
I sacrifice to the public good. I have never whispered
a syllable of them abroad. Within these walls they
were born, and here they shall die. If every one of us
in returning to our Constituents were to report the

objections he has had to it, and endeavor to gain partizans in support of them, we might prevent its being generally received, and thereby lose all the salutary effects & great advantages resulting naturally in our favor among foreign Nations as well as among ourselves, from our real or apparent unanimity.

Much of the strength and efficiency of any Government in procuring and securing happiness to the people, depends, on opinion, on the general opinion [MSNBC? Fox News?] of the goodness of the Government, as well as of the wisdom and integrity of its Governors [except in Illinois, where they'll all go to jail]. I hope therefore that for our own sakes as a part of the people, and for the sake of posterity, we shall act heartily and unanimously in recommending this Constitution (if approved by Congress & confirmed by the Conventions) wherever our influence may extend, and turn our future thoughts & endeavors to the means of having it well administered.

On the whole, Sir, I can not help expressing a wish that every member of the Convention who may still have objections to it, would with me, on this occasion doubt a little of his own infallibility, and to make manifest our unanimity, put his name to this instrument.

The speech worked. Only three delegates refused to sign—Edmund Randolph and George Mason of Virginia and Elbridge Gerry of Massachusetts. Call them our "Founding Stepfathers," and note that their names are not invoked in the same way as those of, for example, Washington or Jefferson. No person or policy is ever deemed "Randolphian," "Masonian," or "Gerrytonian."

George Washington's "Farewell Address" was not an address in the sense of a speech that he gave. It was a "goodbye and good luck" letter to the public published in pamphlet form and in newspapers across the United States in 1796 when Washington had served two terms as president and was adamantly refusing the offer of a third.

Washington was no great prose stylist and knew it. The address was mostly written by Alexander Hamilton (who favored electing a president-for-life). But ghostwriter notwithstanding, the words have a measured, stern, and august tone that is wholly Washingtonian.

The document, at more than six thousand words, is too stately an exercise in eighteenth-century declamation to escape being condensed. What follows is the part most pertinent to current events: Washington's unsparing condemnation of "the spirit of party."

The complete "Farewell Address" contains equally timely warnings against reckless government borrowing, loose interpretations of the Constitution, erosion of the separation of powers, and the kind of nasty regionalism that results in certain Americans being labeled a "basket of deplorables" by someone who not only wasn't offered three terms as president but couldn't even get elected to one.

There is also Washington's often—perhaps too often—cited warning against "foreign alliances, attachments, and intrigues." He was cautioning a new, small, and militarily insignificant nation against involvement in the seemingly never-ending conflict between Britain and France (which started in 1066 and may break out again with Brexit). This is not to say that Washington would have shrugged off the attack on Pearl Harbor or looked askance on NATO membership.

The Father of our Country was not perfectly prescient. But he had a sad and accurate foresight about political faction and all its lies and all its empty promises.

George Washington

Let me now . . . warn you in the most solemn manner against the baneful effects of the spirit of party.

The alternate domination of one faction over another, sharpened by the spirit of revenge natural to party dissension . . . has perpetrated the most horrid enormities [and] is itself a frightful despotism.

But this leads at length to a more formal and permanent despotism. The disorders and miseries which result gradually incline the minds of men to seek security and repose in the absolute power of an individual; and sooner or later the chief of some prevailing faction . . . turns this disposition to the purposes of his own elevation, on the ruins of public liberty.

[Even] without . . . an extremity of this kind . . . the common and continual mischiefs of the spirit of party are sufficient to make it the interest and duty of a wise people to discourage and restrain it.

[The spirit of party] serves always to distract the public councils and enfeeble the public administration. It agitates the community with ill-founded jealousies and false alarms, kindles the animosity of one part against another, foments occasionally riot and insurrection. *It opens the door to foreign influence and corruption, which finds . . . access to the government itself through the channels of party passions.*

[Italics added because—*wow!*—G.W. predicts Russian hackers two hundred years before the Internet was invented.]

[The spirit of party is] a fire not to be quenched, it demands a uniform vigilance to prevent its bursting into a flame, lest, instead of warming, it should consume.

What I Like About U.(S.A.)

Always look on the bright side of life!

—Eric Idle, *Monty Python's Life of Brian*

Three things I like about America are fast food, suburban sprawl, and traffic jams.

The Traffic Jam as Serotonin Reuptake Inhibitor

My own personal form of taking Zoloft is to listen to "Traffic on the 3s" every ten minutes on WBZ Boston news radio, 1030 on my AM dial. Nothing cheers me up more than a Boston traffic jam—when I'm not in it.

I live far and gone in the New England back country where there isn't any traffic. But I get lonely out here, feel isolated and down in the dumps sometimes, especially when New England weather is awful the way it's been this winter, and last winter, and last fall, and last summer, and the way it will be this spring.

Good weather is so rare here that we don't even have a word for it and just stand around with our mouths gaping open, rendered speechless by sunshine.

Anyway, when I get depressed I tune in to the WBZ traffic report, and I'm instantly full of optimism, good feelings, and love of life—compared to the people in Boston who are stuck in traffic. Which would be all of them. WBZ has a slogan for its traffic report: "Boston— it's an hour's drive from Boston."

Why Boston traffic is so bad I don't know. Boston isn't a huge city, less populous in fact than Columbus, Ohio, or Charlotte, North Carolina. And Boston drivers are notoriously aggressive—curb-jumping, left-turning-on-red, one-way wrongwaying lead-foot lane-hopping lions in the zebra crossing.

They should, by all rights, be able to hot rod their way out of any traffic tie-up. (Why don't Boston drivers use turn signals? *That would be giving classified information to the enemy.*)

But Boston has something called the "Leverett Connector." This is where I-93, Rt. 1, Rt. 3, Rt. 28, Storrow Drive, the Charles River, Boston Harbor, the Zakim Bridge, the Rose Kennedy Greenway, and the Callahan Tunnel to Logan Airport all meet. If you're coming into Boston from the north . . . or the south . . . or the east . . . or the west you will end up in the Leverett Connector. You may not mean to but you will.

If you want to go to Faneuil Hall, Old North Church, the Bull and Finch Pub (the bar that inspired *Cheers*), Fenway Park, or a Celtics or Bruins game you'll end up in the Leverett Connector.

Even if you're headed someplace that's nowhere near the Leverett Connector, such as Gillette Stadium, you'll end up in the Leverett Connector. It's the Murphy's Law of driving in a city where a lot of people are named Murphy.

However, if you're *not* in Boston—the way I'm not in Boston—it doesn't matter into what depths of despair you may have fallen. You can turn on WBZ any time night or day, even 5:03 a.m. on a Sunday morning, and hear those wonderful inspiring words that will snap you out of your gloom and put joy back into your heart: "It's a sea of brake lights on the Leverett Connector."

Actually, I like traffic jams even when I am in one. (Though not on the Leverett Connector. People have gone through puberty, grown to adulthood, become middle-aged, and gotten Alzheimer's between the exit from the Zakim Bridge and the entrance to the Callahan Tunnel.)

I like traffic jams because they give me a chance to look at my fellow Americans while they're doing what most defines us as Americans—being stuck in a traffic jam.

And what a land of equal opportunity this is! Seeing hundreds of my fellow countrymen in their cars makes it clear that, in America, no one is too intellectually challenged, differently abled, emotionally fragile, beset by anger management issues, encumbered by dementia, or burdened by obsessive-compulsive disorders involving personal communication devices, burritos, and Grande Caffe Lattes to have a car. (And, presumably, a driver's license.) There may be discrimination in this country but not on the highways.

It's better for everyone that these people are stuck in traffic—you don't want them at home. Traffic jams ensure they'll never get there.

And the cars are interesting. Pickup trucks have grown enormous. (Living in the country, I myself own a pickup, but its model year is 1984.) Today's pickup trucks are full-size four-door luxury sedans except as tall as a house and with doorsills so high that you have to stand on a Prius to get inside. What are these pickup truck drivers picking up? The pickup beds are the size of a backyard aboveground pool and there's never anything in them. Yet, in the next lane over, there will be a Fiat 500 with a mattress and a box spring bungee-corded to the roof, a backseat full of moving cartons and kitchen appliances, and a sectional couch hanging out of the hatchback. Do we need to introduce these folks to each other?

Also, where did minivans go? You see fewer and fewer of them. Almost every family used to have a minivan. They're inexpensive and space efficient with room for six or eight kids in the back and all of their skateboards, terrain park skis, mountain bikes, lacrosse sticks, and a full-size soccer goal net. But minivans seem to have been replaced by much more expensive and much less space efficient SUVs with the kind of off-road capability I had no idea that ordinary parents needed. We know America's average family size is getting smaller. Is it possible that parents are using SUVs to drive their children deep into the wilderness and feed them to wolves?

Suburban Sprawl—Beauty
Is in the Me of the Beholder

I like suburban sprawl because it all looks alike. When we leave our rural home and "go into town," we go to a commercial strip on Rt. 101A in Nashua, New Hampshire. It looks exactly like every other commercial strip in America—same big box stores, gas stations, franchise restaurants, car dealerships, vape shops, nail salons, and hairdressing establishments with "funny" names . . . Curl Up & Dye.

You'd have no idea you were in New England unless you happened to catch sight of the leaves turning orange in the fall on the couple of sickly maples that Target has planted in its parking lot islands. You could be anyplace—Los Angeles, Phoenix, Orlando. This cuts down greatly on travel expenses. No need to take a flight to Los Angeles, Phoenix, or Orlando.

Newspaper op-ed columnists, social critics, stand-up comedians, and other aesthetes often make derisive comments about suburban sprawl being all alike. What's so bad about being all alike? People are alike. Why is it a bad thing when people eat and shop alike? People should be treated the same way no matter their gender, sexual preference, race, ethnicity, or religion. And what's wrong with them being treated the same way at the same big box stores, gas stations, franchise restaurants, car dealerships, vape shops, nail salons, and hairdressing establishments?

Yes, suburban sprawl is ugly. Or is it? I've been to Venice. A great beauty spot, I'm told. All I saw in St. Mark's Square was a waving field of selfie sticks from ten thousand Chinese tourists. The sickly maples in the Target parking lot are scenically glorious by comparison. And just try parking in Venice. There are limits to the off-road capabilities of even the best SUV. Bring your snorkel. (And get a tetanus shot.)

Parking is easy in the suburbs. Everything is easy in the suburbs. It's the best place to grow up. You've got lots of other kids to play with (unless their parents have been feeding them to wolves).

In the suburbs, unlike the city, you've got places to play where you aren't constantly being run over by Uber drivers. And, unlike the country, you've got fresh air and sunshine without your only friend being Lassie, who has to rescue you from a well every week. (I know about these things. We raised our kids in the country and, lacking a collie with a Mensa IQ, had to do it ourselves, standing on the back steps yelling, "Get the @#$% out of the well!")

My only worry about suburban sprawl is that Internet shopping will drive malls out of business. Without malls where will suburban kids hang out? (Kids hate fresh air and sunshine.)

Malls are good places for kids—compared to the Internet. There are no "alt-right" shops at the mall. Alexandria Ocasio-Cortez doesn't have a retail outlet where she sells socialism to young people. The "messaging" at malls is inclusive and all about good old-fashioned capitalism.

There's no porn at the mall, if you don't count Abercrombie & Fitch shopping bags. There's not much that's truly loathsome, unless you hate the Marvel superhero movies at the Cineplex as much as I do. At the mall the scope of evil is pretty much limited to shoplifting. Which is bad. But, according to Barnes & Noble, it's something that Jeff Bezos has been doing for years. Would you rather have your kids hanging out at the mall or hanging out on the Internet? Zara is closed at 2 a.m. when kids are supposed to be asleep. The Internet isn't.

Fast Food—It's Fast and It's Food

Anyone who complains about American fast food is too young or too dumb to recall the greasy spoons that came before franchise restaurants. You'd be driving down the highway, and everybody in the car was hungry, and you'd have to pull over to whatever was along the roadside with a big sign out front that said "Eat and Get Gas."

And, depending on the circumstances, pricier sit-down restaurants aren't necessarily what we want instead of McDonald's. Now that legalized marijuana has become ubiquitous, we can be frank about this. Has anyone ever smoked a joint and had a "foie gras attack"?

Fast food may be contributing to America's obesity problem. But take me to a Michelin three-star French bistro and I'm going to order things that are much more fattening than a Big Mac. Starting with that foie gras and going straight to escargots in garlic butter sauce, roasted duck breast (1,500 calories and 25 grams of fat), asparagus hollandaise, potatoes au gratin, crème brûlée, and a big wedge of cheese washed down with two bottles of 1996 Château Latour. At least when I emerge from between the golden arches I'm just fat, not fat and broke.

Plus some fast food is delicious by any standards— In-N-Out Burger, Chick-fil-A, Whataburger. I fondly remember when that icon of suburban sprawl Popeyes fried chicken first came north. It was in the 1980s, when I lived in New York and was dating a stylish young lady from New Orleans who was full of scorn for Yankee cooking. She claimed a decent meal could not be had north of the Mason-Dixon line. Every few weeks she'd give a dinner party, inviting New York guests for "a real southern treat."

But the stylish young lady could not cook. What she did was sneak down to the only Popeyes in the city, which was in a scary neighborhood on Forty-second Street. She'd come home with her Vera Bradley bag full of spicy white and dark, biscuits, Cajun fries, red beans and rice, and jambalaya. She'd stick them in silver serving dishes and everyone would rave.

It's a Free Country

And I like that. We Americans are supposed to be able to do what we want to do. And what we want to do is obvious. Fifty-two percent of us live in the suburbs. On any given day 37 percent of us will eat fast food. And, as far as I can tell, a hundred percent of us are stuck in a traffic jam on the Leverett Connector.

Acknowledgments

Herewith the part of a book that nobody reads except for the people whose names the author accidentally left out. And me. I'm a fan of "Acknowledgments." Often I'd rather read the acknowledgments than the book in which they appear.

Acknowledgments are informative. If, right at the start, the author thanks someone you've never heard of in lavish terms but for vague reasons, that person is the ghostwriter. And the more lavish (and vague) the gratitude, the less likely it is that the author has read his or her own book that the ghostwriter wrote.

No such person will appear in these acknowledgments, partly because I can't afford one but mostly because even the most mercenary ghostwriters *do* have standards.

Likewise, in nonfiction books, expansive compliments to "research assistants" mean that people more intelligent than the author—not usually hard to find—are responsible for the content. Fulsome praise of a particular research assistant indicates the author and that assistant are having a torrid affair. My lack of research assistants proves (a.) I'm no hunk and (b.) nobody with *any* intelligence is responsible for this content.

Also be alert—in the bibliography as well as the acknowledgments—to authors' long lists of "other works that have made this book possible," especially if those works are little known, out of print, or available only in downloaded microfiche digital images. I'm not saying nonfiction authors are plagiarists. They may also be lying their heads off about having read all that shit.

No plagiarism accusations, however, are to be made against humorists. Why accuse us of something for which we already stand convicted? The whole world knows we'll steal jokes from *anywhere*. No T-shirt slogan, bathroom graffiti, or Snapchat cat meme is safe from our thievery. Although there are a few humorists who are innocent of this crime. The technical term for them, in the humor trade, is "not funny."

Another acknowledgment sentence to be on the look-out for begins, "This book could never have been written without . . ." What follows is usually an encomium to a spouse or partner. What *should* follow is the word "money."

People who don't write for money exist. They include sensitive poets—sensitive to everything except meter and rhyme. Also, old duffers pecking away at personal histories on their Royal portables. The children of the old duffers had better pretend to be thrilled if they want to stay in the will. (I believe a close reading of the First Amendment would indicate that sensitive poets with execrable scansion and old duffers with self-published life stories—along with TikTok rappers, social media influencers, people who use "journal" as a verb, and Donald Trump—are tacitly excluded from the constitutional prohibition against abridging the freedom of speech.)

So let us get to the heart of the matter. This book could never have been written without money from my friend, editor, and long-suffering (having commissioned every book I've ever written) publisher Morgan Entrekin, president of Grove Atlantic.

Morgan paid me money. What he got in return was this book. Call it one of the mysteries of late-stage capitalism. I don't understand late-stage capitalism and, thank God, neither does Morgan.

But let's not forget the encomium to a spouse or partner that usually goes about here in an acknowledgments, in place of vulgar talk of pelf.

In years gone by, when most writers were men and most writers' spouses or partners were wives, what was really meant by the obligatory panegyric was this: "She retyped the whole manuscript including my indecipherable scribbles in the margins and fixed the spelling, punctuation, and grammar. She took care of the house and the kids, cooked all the meals, mowed the lawn, and changed the oil in the car because I was drunk when I wasn't writing and sometimes when I was. She held down a full-time job of her own because this book is six years overdue. She never got nosey and discovered the torrid affair I was having with my research assistant. I'm filing for divorce the minute I cash the check for the movie rights."

Nowadays, of course, writers may be of any gender, their spouses or partners likewise, and their domestic arrangements highly variable. And what modern writers have to say about their spouses or partners is *still a load of crap*.

Look, we're writers. It's what we do. Therefore I will skip the sugared words about you, Tina O'Rourke, and hope that my silence speaks volumes of appreciation, esteem, admiration, obligation, wonder, delight, pride, gratitude, and love (not to mention monogamy).

I would maintain an equally eloquent muteness about the other people I need to thank, but that would mean leaving their names out thereby causing them to read this and learn that writers are deplorable people. Since many of these people work with writers for a living and some are writers themselves, this would be disheartening information.

Thank you everyone at *American Consequences*, the free political economics web magazine where I am editor in chief.

Therefore I have no one but myself to blame for the twenty-four chapters of this book that first appeared in *American Consequences*.

The blame is all mine, but if you, kind reader, find anything creditable in those chapters please give that credit to *AmCon*'s distinguished staff:

Publisher Steven Longenecker—"Publish and be damned," said the Duke of Wellington when a blackmailer threatened to print shocking letters by the Duke. And Steven must sometimes feel the same way about the drafts we *American Consequences* writers dump upon his desk. But he never gives into the temptation to send us to perdition. He keeps the magazine on the straight and narrow path to a blessed publication.

Managing Editor Laura Greaver—she can manage everything and edit anything and manages to edit out managerial noise while managing to add editorial authority to every edition. We don't call her "Managing Editor" for nothing.

Creative Director Erica Wood—an illustrative dream for subjects that are a nightmare to illustrate, a Picasso of pie charts. She brings the light of art to the dismal science of economics. Her bar graphs should hang in the Louvre.

(As I said, *American Consequences* is free. Just Google us, click on "Subscribe," and you will hear from us constantly—the way you constantly hear from other best-things-in-life-free stuff, such as your family.)

And we at *American Consequences* thank our friends at the clear-eyed and far-sighted financial advisory company Stansberry Research. In particular:

Founder Porter Stansberry—Odysseus of the financial seas, navigating between the Scylla of booms and the Charybdis of busts, tied to the mast of wise investment while the Sirens of Wall Street try to lure customers onto the rocks of fatal debt and equity portfolios.

General Manager Jamison Miller—as in Five-Star General. Jamison is Eisenhower planning the investment newsletter D-Day, which is every day because they're daily newsletters invading the hard-fought market beachheads each morning. What's more, Jamison is also in charge of making work fun—something Ike notably failed to accomplish on June 6, 1944.

Many of the chapters in this book were inspired by Stansberry Research insights and analysis, and "The Inaugural Address I'd Like to Hear" was originally published in the *Stansberry Digest*.

A briefer version of the preface and the chapters "It's Time to Make Rich People Uncomfortable Again" and "A License to Drive (Me Crazy)" were first published in the opinion pages of the *Washington Post* under the aegis of Associate Op-Ed Editor Mark Lasswell. Mark is the Clark Kent of the *Post*, yanking off his horn-rims and dashing into phone booths and emerging dressed (metaphorically, I hope) in cape and tights to save the world . . . from my clumsy prose, among other grave threats.

"Woke to the Sound of Laughter" was published by Freddy Gray, editor of *Spectator USA*. Well done, Freddy, for letting me take a whack at the puzzling gestures of virtue signaling, but, even more, for finally importing the *Spectator*, published weekly in Britain since 1828, to America, a country with high tariff barriers on intelligence and wit. Freddy, I can only hope that your use of polysyllabic words, references to obscure authors such as Shakespeare, and occasional failure to remove the "u" from color and harbor do not impede your success in America's marketplace of ideas, such as it is.

For almost forty years, my lecture agency, GTN, a UTA company, has been—try to wrap your head around this—convincing people to *pay* to listen to me talk. I wish GTN were in charge of my household. I'd be getting an allowance from the kids instead of the other way around, and I'd have all the dogs' Milk-Bones. But the really great thing would be the *listening*. Thanks to GTN I've experienced a lot of it at venues all around the country. But it's never happened to me at home.

(BTW, proposed new business model for GTN suggested by my kids and dogs: convincing people to pay me to shut up.)

Thanks to GTN team members Debbie Greene, Kristen Sena, Jen Peykar, and most of all David Buchalter. Put Debbie, Kristen, Jen, and David on the case and they'd have Neil deGrasse Tyson addressing the annual meeting of the Flat Earth Society, Greta Thunberg lecturing OPEC, Dick Cheney giving a PowerPoint presentation to PETA, and Alexandria Ocasio-Cortez making the keynote speech at Davos.

And don't get me started on GTN founder Don Epstein. His genius is not only in finding audiences for speakers but in coaching and cajoling those speakers into becoming brilliant public orators. Don is so good at it that, if wise heads had prevailed in certain political campaign staffs and Don had been consulted, Mike Bloomberg would have turned into the Demosthenes of Democrats and Bill Weld would have become the Win-One-for-the-Gipper of the GOP, and Mike and Bill would be running neck-and-neck in the 2020 presidential election.

Then there is the matter of public relations. An author wants a book to have a public. And an author wants that public to have a relationship with the book that's something more intimate than Swipe Left. This is where the astute skills and discerning perceptions of Scott Manning & Associates come into play. Founder Scott Manning and his colleague Abigail Welhouse are fabulous relationship counselors. They sit down with the public and the book. They urge the public to talk through its insecurities and anxieties about the book and be more sensitive to the book's needs. They advise the book to be more supportive of the public and more open to emotional engagement. They help the public and the book build a relationship that is so strong, enduring, and mutually respectful that even a $26 cover price doesn't cause screaming and tears and slammed doors.

But, of course, all of the foregoing thanks would be "thanks for nothing" if it weren't for the people at Grove Atlantic who made this book a physical reality.

And a thing of beauty, as all Grove Atlantic books are. This is the work of Art Director Gretchen Mergenthaler who has turned our hardcovers and paperbacks into fashion statements. Don't wear Givenchy, don't wear Dolce & Gabbana, don't wear Prada, don't wear Ralph Lauren, carry a Grove Atlantic book. In fact don't wear anything at all. Just carry a Grove Atlantic book and you'll be dressed for . . . well, that depends on the subject of the individual book. In the case of my book you'll have a beautiful fig leaf to clothe your ideological nakedness when you're expelled from the political Garden of Eden for having tasted the fruit of the tree of knowledge of good and evil. Or that's what I'd like to think. Anyway, the fig leaf will look good on you.

The job of Managing Editor Julia Berner-Tobin and Production Director Sal Destro is—authors being the irresponsible and self-willed creatures that we are—to herd cats. They are good at it. If Julia and Sal had been cowpokes in the wild west, the Chisholm Trail would have been crowded with thousands of cats, all moving north at a steady pace in an orderly fashion from the litter boxes of Texas to the scratching posts of Abilene.

Copyeditor Donald Kennison is the SEAL Team Six of semicolons, the Clausewitz of subordinate clauses, the Sun Tzu of syntax, and the Washington at the Valley Forge of my tangled sentence structure.

Director of Publicity Deb Seager is so good at publicizing things that she could get a front-page headline out of a Dalmatian having spots, set off a Twitter storm over the Pope being Catholic, and cause the House Judiciary Committee to hold a congressional hearing about where bears go to the bathroom.

Associate Publisher Judy Hottensen is responsible for sales. "Could sell ice to Eskimos" is no longer an acceptable cliché in these times of climate change and heightened sensitivity to language. (Although soon someone may well need to market Sub-Zeros to the Inuit.) So let us instead say that Judy could sell dial phones to Tim Cook, Sears and Roebuck catalogues to Jeff Bezos, and a complete set of *The World Book* to Wikipedia.

Editorial Assistant Sara Vitale is learning just how much assistance authors need, especially if they're of a certain age. Sara, I know you're hundreds of miles away in New York, but where the heck are my car keys?

And, lastly, let me return to the aforementioned Morgan Entrekin. If James Joyce had had the advantage of Morgan's blue pencil, *Finnegans Wake* would have been at the top of the *New York Times* bestseller list every week since 1939.

And if all publishing houses were run like Grove Atlantic, the whole world would have its face in a book instead of an LCD screen. Smartphones would be used as nothing but bookmarks. Even the character who's been hanging out in the TV room at 1600 Pennsylvania Avenue for the past four years would become a bookworm. (Morgan, can we get the reprint rights for a large print edition of *Go the Fuck to Sleep*?)